MONEY Rules

JULIETTE FAIRLEY

FOREWORD BY
STEPHEN M. POLLAN

Prentice
Hall Press

Library of Congress Cataloging-in-Publication Data

Fairley, Juliette
    Money Rules: personal finance strategies for your 20s and 30s / Juliette Fairley.
        p. cm.
    ISBN 0-7352-0236-2
    1. Generation X—United States—Finance, Personal.   2. Finance, Personal—United States.
    3. Investments—United States.   I. Title.

HG179 .F327 2001
332.024--dc21   00-053049

Acquisitions Editor: Luis Gonzalez
Production Editor: Mariann Hutlak
Interior Design: Nicola Evans
Composition: DM Cradle Associates

This publication is designed to provide accurate and authoritative information in regard to
the subject matter covered. It is sold with the understanding that the publisher is not engaged
in rendering legal, accounting, or other professional service. If legal advice or other expert
assistance is required, the services of a competent professional person should be sought.
*—From the Declaration of Principles jointly adopted by a Committee of the American Bar
Association and a Committee of Publishers and Associations.*

Printed in the United States of America
10 9 8 7 6 5 4 3 2 1

ISBN 0-7352-0236-2

ATTENTION: CORPORATIONS AND SCHOOLS

Prentice Hall Press books are available at quantity discounts with bulk purchase for educational,
business, or sales promotional use. For information, please write to: Prentice Hall Direct Special
Sales, 240 Frisch Court, Paramus, NJ 07652. Please supply: title of book, ISBN, quantity, how the
book will be used, date needed.

 **Prentice Hall Press** Paramus, NJ 07652

http://www.phdirect.com

SEIGNEUR

JE TE REMERCIE

CONTENTS

FOREWORD BY STEPHEN M. POLLAN

CHAPTER 1

LIFE AND MONEY IN YOUR 20S AND 30S—THE GENERATION X LANDSCAPE

CHAPTER 4

BANKING: THE BASICS AND BEYOND

CHAPTER 5

INSURANCE

CHAPTER 6

INVESTING

CHAPTER 8

INDIVIDUAL RETIREMENT ACCOUNTS

CHAPTER 9

GETTING CLEAR ON 401(K) PLANS

CHAPTER 15

BUYING A HOME

CHAPTER 16

TAX TIPS

ACKNOWLEDGMENTS

A book takes on a life of its own once you start to write one. *Money Rules* gathered its own momentum and people came out of the woodwork to help. It would have been twice as difficult to fulfill my destiny of writing this book without certain people whom either helped with charts, research, blurbs, interviews, advice, or just good old-fashioned support.

They include Maude Divittis at MTV, Diann Witt at NYU, Cynthia Simpson at Beliefnet.com, Ashton Newhall, Steve Norwitz at T. Rowe Price, Stephanie Flanagan, John Collins at the ICI, Reggie Greiner, Karen Metzger, Andrew Totolos, Linda Barlow, Rodney Brooks at *USA Today*, Doug Rogers at *Investor's Business Daily*, Eric Scholl at Yahoo, David Bennett, Timothy Martin, Jaye Smith, Janet Briaud, Jonas Ferris, Thaddeus Wong, Larry Tabak, Sue Herrera at CNBC, Matt Coffin, Annie Jennings PR, Russell Hall, Ted David at CNBC, Bob Pickett, Mallary Tytel, Nick Chiles, Pamela Toussaint, Christopher Jones at Financial Engines, Stewart Welch, Seth Cohen, Howard Dvorkin, Chris Cummin, Bernard Frelat, Anna Morgan, Caroline Shirzadi, the producers at "Curtis Court TV," producers at "Good Day NY," Jeremy French, Gregg Bleakney, Ed McCoyd, Stephen Pollan,

Richard Greene, Victoria Collins, Igor Bass, Kevin McKeon, Bambi Holzer, Bob Saba at Cyberdialogue, Ann Piacentini at Scudder Kemper Investments, M. Eileen Dorsey, Joe Wisniewski, Tom Foster, Durant Abernathy, Mike Staten, Barbara Corcoran, Janet Quinn Wise, Jim Neuwirth, Jennifer Cardoza, William O'Shea, Jeff Close, the CFP Board, Jennifer Frighetto at Hewitt & Associates, the National Center for Education Statistics, Aurora D'Amico, Forum for Investor Advice, Chris Lawler at SRI Consulting, Lillian Ayala at Uniworld Group, Oppenheimer Funds, Jim Broderick at Datek, Tom Taggart and Brad Zigler at Barclays Global, Kelvin Boston, Wadene Howard, Bill W., Peter Shankman, Bernardo, Eric Davis, Glinda Bridgforth, the Author's Guild, Mom and Dad, Simon Taffler, John May, Dr. Carmen Maza, Debra Larsen at TechSpace, Andrew Sernovitz at GasPedal, New York Business Forums, Bob Casey at Bloomberg Wealth Manager, Matt Cassin, Tony Seidl, Larry Cohen, Owen Davis, Robert Levitan, Jack Hidary, Dave Morgan, Don Gabor, Bob Frare, Diahann Lassus, the Stern Marketing Group, George Wu, Karl Weber, Roger Smith, Russell Hall, Michelle Allen, the Gran Ventana, Robin Richards Donohoe, Darnell Williams, Suzanne King, John Neis, Wyc Grosbeck, Patty Abramson, Doug Morriss, Justin Segal, Guy Kawasaki, Arkansas Financial Group, Shannon Ryan, Dave Snyder and Eric Goldberg at the American Insurance Association, Southerlyn Marino, Vin Cipolla, Sherry Abbott, Dr. Steve Batson, Mindy Kobrin, Arlynn Greenbaum, Natasha Strauss at New York City Inner City Games, Ray Javdan, Terry Hines for legal advice, Jack Dolan and Herb Perone at ACLI, Kiva Kolstein, Shaun Manchand, Lois Katz at MSNBC, Mary Duffy, Mark Oldman, Linda Powers, Venetia Kontogouris.

The team at Prentice Hall Press: Ellen Schneid Coleman, Yvette Romero, Lisa Giassa, Mariann Hutlak, and Eugene Brissie, who bought the book in the first place. Please bring it to my attention if I have forgotten you, I will include you in the next book! Thanks to you all. Love, Juliette.

FOREWORD

Money, not sex, is the ultimate taboo. While presidential peccadilloes are openly discussed by family and friends, personal salary and income are never mentioned. Children are taught the facts of life, but not the facts of money. As a result, most of us grow up with financial lives that mirror our neuroses rather than our hopes and dreams.

Money Rules is a fabulous antidote to this illness. In a voice that's authoritative without being condescending, and a manner that's serious without being somber, it can help young people keep from repeating the mistakes of their elders. *Money Rules* breaks the cycle of financial dysfunction and codependency that has made so many people monetary cripples.

While *Money Rules* may end up cutting into my own future earnings as a financial consultant, I can't help but admire the way it steers readers toward prudent steps, in their 20s and 30s, and beyond. Whether it's explaining how to exploit the magic of compound interest, the significance of setting up IRAs and contributing to 401(k)s—whether or not you ever plan on retiring—or the importance of not going into debt, *Money Rules* provides essential counsel.

Rather than just a translation of traditional financial advice into Gen X language, *Money Rules* addresses the specific needs and wants of those in their 20s and 30s. It suggests not accepting money from parents when first starting out unless it's a documented loan. It stresses keeping separate accounts when moving in with a lover. It urges readers to finance vacations through regular saving rather than using a windfall, such as a tax refund. It explains how important it is to make sure potential roommates aren't financial flakes. It offers alternative ways to come up with a down payment for a home or apartment.

All this information is presented in a cutting-edge package as well. Along with the advice of financial planners are the tales of Gen Xers themselves. Supplementing the text are checklists and bullet points and tips that can serve as guideposts for readers marking their progress to money mastery.

Making money is central to success in the 21st century. Money may not buy you happiness, but the lack of money will certainly buy you unhappiness. Money does indeed, rule. And *Money Rules* is the Gen Xers essential guidebook.

Stephen M. Pollan

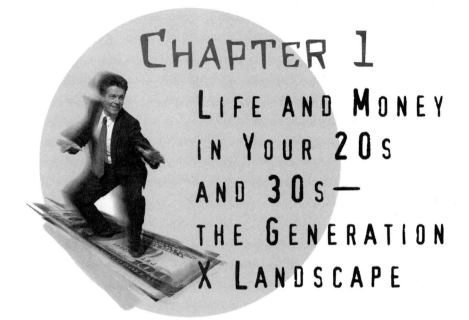

CHAPTER 1

LIFE AND MONEY IN YOUR 20s AND 30s— THE GENERATION X LANDSCAPE

NOT YOUR FATHER'S PERSONAL FINANCE

LIFE AND MONEY ISSUES FOR THOSE OF US IN OUR 20S AND 30S— Generation X (Gen X)—are different from those of our parents. Our approach and attitude towards personal finance and investing can be different as well. Take George Wu, for example. At 34, he works as a senior manager in the marketing industry in Oakland, California. He invests in the Internet, his 401(k) plan, and mutual funds on the side. His philosophy towards investing is "do-it-yourself."

"My feeling is that there isn't one particular resource out there which can provide me with a comprehensive approach. So, I might as well do it myself through research," he says.

Wu also holds a typical belief about Social Security. "I don't think there will be a whole lot there when I retire. It's nice to hear that we have a budget surplus right now, but I don't know how that will be optimized so that Gen X will participate in Social Security," says Wu.

Wu's philosophy about Social Security and his do-it-yourself attitude about investing reflect Generation Xers' self-reliant and self-sufficient tendencies. Remember, many of us come from single-parent homes, or homes where both mother and father worked. Most of us, therefore, probably learned to be self-reliant at an early age.

OUR UNIQUE SET OF ISSUES

While we could turn to our parents for advice on investing and personal finance, we are not likely to do so. Part of the reason is our self-reliant nature. More important, however, the circumstances surrounding our generation as they pertain to personal finance are quite different from those faced by our moms and dads. So, what may have made sense for our parents may not be the best approach for us.

Some of the unique financial issues facing Generation X include the uncertainty of Social Security benefits during retirement, an overdependence on technology stocks, the desire to retire early, the inevitability of living longer in retirement because of advances in medical care, the advent of the Internet and its effect on investing, and the availability of 401(k) plans.

THE UNCERTAINTY OF SOCIAL SECURITY

Social Security has a huge surplus from which to pay out benefits, but the government keeps borrowing from it for other purposes, depleting those funds. Some experts say that it will still be around in the next century, but not distributing as much to retirees and starting later than age 65. Others say that Social Security will be bankrupt by 2030. That's because baby boomers will be retiring in record numbers. There are an estimated 76 million baby boomers born between 1946 and 1964 who are expected to collect Social Security benefits in the first quarter of this century. Some say that boomers will bankrupt the system before we Gen Xers even have a chance to apply for benefits.

Most would agree the future of Social Security is uncertain at best. According to a survey by Scudder Kemper Investments, 46% of Gen Xers said that they felt they are unlikely to receive any benefits, and another 33% felt they might receive reduced benefits.

This harsh reality means we will have to do much of our own saving for retirement. This is especially true since companies have all but stopped offering pension plans, leaving the burden of accumulating retirement funds on the shoulders of employees. We will have to save more money for retirement than any other generation before us. We will have to be financially savvy about our options, which include 401(k) plans and IRAs.

FIGURE 1–1   Perspective on Social Security

	Gen X	Baby Boomers	Swing	GI/ WWII
Will likely receive full benefits	10%	20%	53%	68%
Will likely receive reduced benefits	33%	(50%)	34%	17%
Not likely to receive any benefits	(46%)	23%	6%	3%
No opinion	12%	7%	7%	11%

Source: Scudder Kemper Investments

RETIRING EARLY

Recent surveys show that most Gen Xers plan to retire at 60 years old or younger. But we often don't know what it will take to do that. Experts say that Gen Xers will need about $3,000,000 to retire comfortably—that's considerably more than the $1,000,000 needed for those retiring today.

LIVING LONGER

One of the reasons we will need more money in retirement than previous generations is that we are expected to live longer, given increased longevity due to advances in medical care.

Instead of passing away in our 70s (as is the case with life expectancy today), Gen Xers are expected to have average life spans of 90 years or more. In some cases, we will live longer in retirement than when we were employed.

THE INTERNET

As with so many other aspects of our lives, the Internet is revolutionizing the way we go about our personal finances and investing. For everything from online banking to investing online, researching investment opportunities, and day trading, the Internet is an ideal tool for those of us who like to do it ourselves.

This is all well and good, but the flip side is that the ease with which we can research investment options and trade stocks on the Internet can also give us what might be a false sense of knowledge about investing. Needless to say, we need to be both savvy and cautious.

TECHNOLOGY STOCKS— THE MAGIC FORMULA?

Gen Xers have been big believers in technology stocks, even during those times when tech stocks have had lackluster performance, because we grew up during times of great technological advancement. Since we rely on the Internet for so many of our daily activities, we put a lot of faith in the value of technology companies.

But this overdependence on technology stocks can lead to a lack of diversification in our portfolios. The danger of not being diversified is if tech stocks take a dive, the entire portfolio goes down with it, leaving no other sector as a buffer to keep the portfolio buoyant.

Diahann Lassus, a certified financial planner in New Providence, New Jersey, says that about 15% of her clientele are Generation Xers.

> *"With one 30-year-old client, it's like pulling teeth to get him to invest in anything but technology stocks because he thinks that's the future, and why should he invest in anything else," says Lassus. "But we all know that diversification is still very important and you can't ignore it."*

THE ERA OF THE 401(k)

The 401(k) plan was introduced to the American public in 1981. This was right at the time companies stopped offering pension plans to their employees. Gen Xers were among the first to take advantage of the 401(k) plan.

For many Gen Xers, the 401(k) plan was their first exposure to the concept of investing for the future. According to a recent survey, most of us are making use of our 401(k) plans. Yet, the same survey shows, many are not taking full advantage of the plan by contributing the maximum. As we'll discuss later in the book, maximizing our 401(k) is one of the key strategies to making the most of our money.

WHICH GEN XER ARE YOU?

Discussed above are some of the life and money issues we all face as Gen Xers. But within our generation, we can find ourselves at different stages. A Gen Xer who is 22, for instance, is probably facing different issues than the Gen Xer who is 34. To illustrate the point, let's explore the following three scenarios:

SCENARIO 1: THE RECENT COLLEGE GRADUATE

The Gen Xer who is just graduating from college is probably facing a mountain of debt. That debt is more than likely student loans and credit card debt. These days, credit card companies are setting up booths at college campuses to attract consumers before they even get into the job market. So, debt will be a big issue for this segment of the Gen X population.

In addition, this age group is probably grappling with the issue of cutting ties with parents and establishing living situations with roommates. In some cases, they are living on their own for the very first time. This may be the first time they are filing taxes. In the past, their parents probably claimed them as a dependent. They are probably starting their first jobs and just finding out what the workplace is all about.

This segment may also be spending frivolously on CDs and designer clothes, when in actuality, this is the time they should start investing their disposable income. Recent college graduates have time on their side. Now is the time they should start investing to take advantage of compounding interest.

SCENARIO 2: HIP AND SINGLE

The Gen Xer between the ages of 26 and 30 is probably single and dating and just getting the hang of worklife. They live for vacations and are scouring for good get-away deals.

They've gotten hip to the wiles of worklife and are looking for ways to deviate. Some interesting areas of conversation for them include sabbaticals, entrepreneurship, and telecommuting. They may also have realized that one of the ways to increase their salary is to job hop. So, many may be interested in transferring retirement plan assets. They may have accumulated a substantial amount in their 401(k) plan and may be thinking about borrowing from it to buy or lease a new car.

The Gen Xers in this segment are probably filing their own taxes electronically and dabbling with investing online. They are still young enough to be seeking fun, but old enough to start thinking about saving for retirement. They may still be sleeping on a futon, but seriously wondering about life and health insurance.

SCENARIO 3: NEWLYWED AND HOUSE-HUNTING

These Gen Xers are between the ages of 30 and 34 and probably spent some time living together before taking the walk down the aisle. They are serious investors and are looking to buy their first home.

They are just now starting to feel comfortable with their lot in life, and are seeking to improve it through investing or starting a business. They are seriously thinking about retirement and may even enlist the help of a financial planner to help them come up with a retirement plan, someone to help them "do it themselves," if you will.

For the first time, they are facing the reality of their parents' inevitable demise. So, they may be interested in issues of elder care and estate planning.

In their marriages, Gen Xers are dealing with combining their assets and negotiating money within their relationship.

How <u>Money Rules</u> Can Help

You've no doubt caught glimpses of yourself and the money-related challenges you face in the scenarios depicted above. Some of it can seem downright scary. Not to worry. *Money Rules* will walk you through the myriad of personal finance issues that are relevant for our generation. You'll find sound, practical advice tailor-made for Gen Xers.

We'll cover everything from living with a roommate to switching jobs; getting the most from your 401(k) to avoiding pitfalls when investing; the DO's and DON'Ts of love and money; strategies for reducing debt and repairing credit; getting the best deal on vacations, buying a home, saving for retirement, and much more. Throughout the book you'll find stories of real-life Gen Xers and the money situations they face. Some will amuse you, others will shock you, but all will offer valuable lessons.

Getting the most from your life and money in your 20s and 30s is what *Money Rules* is all about. So let's get started.

CHAPTER 2
ON YOUR OWN

DEALING WITH PARENTS
AND MONEY

WHETHER YOU'RE LEAVING COLLEGE OR YOUR PARENT'S HOME TO EMBARK upon your own journey in life, adjusting to the expectations of the world and standing solo can be frightening and emotionally taxing. It can also be financially grueling.

You may feel the need to lean on your parents for support, but before you ask to borrow money, consider that there may be strings attached. Most moms and dads are more than happy to see their kids on their own because it means they'll have more money for themselves. But, some parents use money to control their adult children.

Realize that if you borrow money from the people who raised you, there may be a price to pay. For one thing, you never truly learn to handle financial situations on your own or to cope with your mistakes. Second, when you accept money, you become beholden to your parents. In other words, you *owe* them. Even if they say the loan or gift comes without ties, just assume it does. For some, that means loss of independence—reporting back to mom and dad every single detail of your life.

If they insist on helping you out (or if you really need the money), discuss the details with them so that each party is aware of the others' expectations.

Before you take any significant amount of money from Mom and Dad, it is a good idea to draw up a document detailing the loan amount. It can be a two-sentence document stating whether or not it is an interest-bearing loan. Most parents won't charge interest; but some do. Don't balk if they charge you interest; a percentage deal teaches you responsibility. Hopefully, the interest they charge will be a lot less than the bank. At least with interest, your parents won't feel they are being taken. After all, the money they are lending to you could be compounding and gathering interest in their bank or mutual fund account. So, have a heart! Both parties should sign the document. Pay them back even if it means setting up a monthly payment plan.

LIVING WITH A ROOMMATE

If you're like most Gen Xers just starting out, you'll probably want a roommate for your first apartment. Not only can it be scary living alone for the first time, but it can also strap you financially if you have to pay a high rent. Before signing a lease with someone, be realistic. Don't necessarily expect that you'll be living with your best friend or that you'll be chummy with your roommate. Look at a roommate situation as a business arrangement in order to protect yourself.

Perhaps, you've learned something about having roommates in college. If you had the roommate from *hell* in college, then you probably know a little bit about detachment. Unlike college, however, in the real world you can choose your roommate. So, make sure you don't pick a financial flake. One way to screen financial flakes before they move in is to socialize with them at least twice. It doesn't have to be anything extravagant. Perhaps, you grab a cup of coffee at Starbucks, a drink at a trendy bar or invite them to a party.

Five Signs of a Financial Flake

1. Your potential roommate borrows money from you.
2. You learn that he or she is running from creditors.
3. They bum cigarettes because they don't have cash to buy their own pack.
4. He is dodging calls from his former roommate.
5. She's forgotten her wallet or tells you that she had her wallet stolen, leaving you to pay the bill.

Once you've decided on a roommate, communication is the most important part from a psychological standpoint. You need to be very clear about who pays for what. Address the following questions:

- If one room is larger than the other, do you get a discount for the smaller room?
- Do you share food or have separate shelves in the fridge?
- Who pays the electricity bill?
- Who is going to buy the couch?
- Who is going to buy the television?
- Who is going to use what?

Work out a budget that you are both responsible for. For example, if expenses in the apartment cost $1,000, each of you should contribute $500 to pay bills.

Issues will come up. Eventually, you and roomie will get into an argument about the phone bill, the cable TV bill, or who is going to pay what. For example, one person may be a compulsive eater and gobble up all the food. The other person may be appalled. The only way to solve that is to communicate. Draw up an agreement in writing aside from the lease. In this document, detail who is paying for the phone bill, the cable bill, and whether you split expenses down the middle. Both parties sign it. State that the agreement can be canceled if changes need to be made, but there should be something in writing at all times.

Include in the document the food arrangement. Decide whether you're going to the grocery store together and splitting 50/50.

What happens if somebody's boyfriend (girlfriend) is over a lot on the weekends? Discuss how to handle guests within your roommate arrangement ahead of time.

A GENERATION X STORY

Andrew Totolos, a 30-year-old systems manager at an Internet company, used to be a moocher until he got sued.

His girlfriend lived in an apartment with a roommate. Totolos lived there rent-free for two months after his girlfriend split. Totolos stayed in the apartment because she was supposed to come back, but she never did. He moved out. A year later, Totolos received an ominous letter in the mail.

"I was being sued for $700 in back rent for this place by my ex-girlfriend's roommate. I ignored it, just threw the letter away because I figured, 'What are they going to do, arrest me?' " Totolos said.

In response to the letter, he left a nasty message on the roommate's answering machine, which said, "Hey Mary, this is Andrew. I got your letter. I don't have any money today and I'm not going to have any money tomorrow so leave me alone. Why don't you consider it an expensive lesson learned."

Soon, Totolos received a phone call from Judge Mills Lane, the bald guy on TV whose motto is "Let's get it on." They invited Totolos to settle his dispute on national television. In exchange, they would pay the bill if he lost and give him $300 for being on the show.

"We get on the air. She tells her story. I tell my story. The Judge is yelling at both of us, but there was no lease tying me to that apartment. So, I think I am doing a pretty good job here," Totolos said. "But then the judge brings in a tape of the message I left on her machine. I had no idea that she would save it. So they play this tape on the air and it makes me look like the biggest demon devil that ever walked the face of the planet. I was dead in the water." Totolos, a reformed moocher, says he learned that you can be tried for your morals in court.

"I haven't mooched since that point. I can tell you that much. It was actually a wake up call. It made me much more independent than I was at that time," Totolos concluded.

So, what if you're on the receiving end of a moocher in a roommate situation? Speak up right away. State the truth (leave emotion out of it): *Your boyfriend is here all the time. It bugs me for the following reasons: I don't have privacy and he eats up the food. We need to come to a solution on this.*

Be honest, up front, and hold on to an outdated answering machine with the microcassette recording device in it!

BUYING A CAR

Unless you live in a major city with reliable public transportation, you'll need a car. This is one of the largest expenses most Generation Xers will have starting out. Buying a car is the perfect opportunity to build a credit rating and to learn how to manage debt. Ideally, buy yourself an inexpensive new car for $10,000 or under. (Yes, you can buy a new car for under $10,000!) New cars are better than used; at least you know the car is straight off the lot and doesn't have anything wrong with it. The problem with used cars is you may wind up with a lemon that sends you in and out of the car shop, which will end up costing you as much as if you'd paid for a new car.

Once you've paid off the car, don't trade it in immediately. Instead, put away the car payment money in a savings account. The idea is to save enough money to buy your next car in cash. That will save you interest and finance charges.

PAYING YOUR TAXES

Perhaps you are filing your own taxes for the first time. Fret not. If you're like most people between the ages of 22 and 35, your tax situation isn't too complicated yet! Unless you own a business or are self-employed, do your own taxes. This is a good way of becoming familiar with the way the system works, the implications of taxes, and how you can influence your own treasury situation.

Sure, accountants and tax services are there to do it for you. Later in life, it may very well be worth it to hire someone to do it for you. But you save $150 by doing it yourself in the meantime. Filing taxes these days is as easy as picking up the phone or dialing up on a modem with the IRS's e-filing system.

The benefits of e-filing are that you get a faster refund, more accurately processed return, and quick electronic confirmation that the return has been filed. You also have the option of filing both federal and state returns at the same time.

You can file electronically several ways. One way is to go to a tax preparer who is an authorized provider. The tax accountant or preparer completes your return on computer and transmits it directly to the IRS. You can

"An unscrupulous tax preparer may file a fraudulent return, getting you a refund that you may not be entitled to and taking a cut of that. What we recommend is that you choose a preparer the way you would a doctor or lawyer. Be careful. Ask for references from a trusted friend or relative who has used the preparer before," says Kevin McKeon, Communications Manager for the IRS Brooklyn District.

find a list of authorized tax preparers in the phone book, but beware of unscrupulous tax preparers.

If you go with an authorized IRS tax preparer, McKeon says you're pretty safe because the tax preparers who get into the program have to pass a suitability check. "We make sure they have a clean record. We monitor the program to make sure the returns coming in are accurate, and there is a screening process," says McKeon.

Another e-filing option would be using your home computer and a modem to file your return any time of day, 24 hours a day through a third-party transmitter. Go to www.IRS.gov for a listing of online service providers that conduct electronic filing for the IRS. Instead of walking down the street and going to the tax preparer nearest you, you are entering the return yourself on the computer, connecting with a third-party tax preparer, and that tax preparer transmits your data to the IRS. In some cases the service is free or anywhere between $30 and $70. The free online providers are listed on the IRS website. Just click on electronic services.

The third way to e-file is by phone, which is called Telefile. Using a push button phone, you can transmit your tax return to the IRS by entering your W2 information and any 1099 information that you have for interest and savings. To be eligible, you would receive a special tax package in the mail with a personal identification number.

As the chart below shows, the number of individual returns filed electronically is expected to grow considerably over the next few years.

FIGURE 2–1   Calendar Year Projections of Electronically Filed Individual Returns to be Filed 2000–2007 for the United States *(in millions)*

Year	Tele-File	On-Line Filing	Practitioner e-file	Total Individual e-file
1998 Actual	6.0	0.9	17.7	24.6
1999 Estimated	5.7	2.5	21.2	29.3
2000	5.9	4.0	23.7	33.6
2001	6.1–6.5	5.2–6.1	26.7–28.7	38.0–41.4
2002	6.3–6.9	6.1–7.4	28.7–31.3	41.2–45.6
2003	6.5–7.2	7.0–8.4	30.6–33.7	44.1–49.4
2004	6.7–7.6	7.7–9.2	32.4–36.1	46.8–52.9
2005	6.9–8.0	8.6–10.2	34.2–38.5	49.6–56.6
2006	7.1–8.4	9.4–11.1	36.0–40.9	52.5–60.4
2007	7.4–8.8	10.3–12.1	37.8–43.4	55.5–64.3

Source: Internal Revenue Service

CHAPTER 3
LIFE, MONEY, AND WORK

THE WORKING LIFE: THE GENERATION X PERSPECTIVE

MONEY RULES IS ABOUT LIFE AND MONEY IN YOUR 20S AND 30S. AS Gen Xers, we are known for placing at least as much (if not more) value on *quality of life* as financial rewards when it comes to employment situations.

Other generations have referred to us as slackers. To be sure, our perspective on what work should be, and how it fits in with the rest of our lives, is typically different from that of baby boomers. But, for the most part, we are not slackers. Gen Xers share the work ethic of generations before us, but we generally want something more.

Businesses large and small are beginning to offer their employees more flexibility and additional benefits in recognition of the quality-of-life issues that concern so many Gen Xers and others. Yet, many companies will pay lip service to quality of life, but put few policies of that kind into practice.

That is why many Gen Xers, especially those just getting out of college, are apprehensive about diving into a full-time job within corporate America. The fear is getting stuck in a position that pays the bills, but offers few, if any, other rewards.

GETTING YOUR FEET WET: TEMP EMPLOYMENT

A good way to ease into the working life and test the waters is through temporary (temp) positions. Some companies, such as MTV, have long-term temp work programs.

> *"We may need temp workers a couple days a week or for short-term assignments. We may rotate them to different areas based on need if someone goes on vacation or if someone is on a leave of absence. That seems to be a nice way for them to integrate into the organization," says Maude Divittis, a human resources expert at MTV Network's Center for Education and Training.*

Temping is a great opportunity for you to examine the employer while they examine you, and neither party has made a long-term commitment or investment.

After you've temped a couple of years, you may have a better idea of what kind of permanent job you want. You have work experience under your belt, which in turn means you are more likely to get the job you want because you've learned the ropes in corporate America.

BEFORE TAKING YOUR FIRST PERMANENT JOB

Before accepting your first permanent job, take its temperature. Consider what the job entails, its compensation, the corporate culture, and the people with whom you will be working. As you think about the immediate implications of each of these elements, you also need to think about your long-term goals.

WHAT THE JOB ENTAILS

First and foremost, make sure that you understand and are comfortable with what will be asked of you. That is, be sure you feel qualified for the tasks at hand, that you will be willing to do any unpleasant chores or grunt work that may be required, and that you find some fulfillment in at least part of your duties.

You should also make sure, however, that you will have ample opportunity for acquiring new skills and knowledge.

"View your job as a stepping stone to something else, then really map it out by saying, 'O.K., in the next job that I want, I will have to know this or that.' Acquire those skills to get to that step," says Diann Witt, assistant director of the Center for Career Education and Life Planning at New York University's School of Continuing and Professional Studies.

Of course, your current job may not always provide all the "on-the-job training" you need for your next position. Jaye Smith, a managing director at a human resources consulting firm, says, "If you have to invest in yourself by taking courses outside the job, do it."

COMPENSATION

Your starting point with compensation is: How much money will you need in order to get by? Avoid jobs that pay so poorly you would need to rely on family or friends for financial assistance. At the same time, don't necessarily jump at the highest offer if other circumstances don't seem right.

Once you've settled on a position, see if you have some room to negotiate your salary. Be reasonable, of course, but also keep in mind that your starting salary sets the tone for future compensation.

Since money isn't the sole factor in attracting younger workers, companies are becoming more creative in what they do for employees. For example, it's not audacious for you to work out a deal trading an increase in salary for more vacation time. Or, during the interviewing process, you may demand a sabbatical after five years so that you can go abroad to study a foreign language.

> *"I think the Xer needs to really do an evaluation of what is important to them, and chances are the company may be willing to do something to tailor a plan to fit what their needs are, whether it is job sharing, flexible hours or staggering the hours that people come in," says NYU's Diann Witt.*

CORPORATE CULTURE

We are not talking here about *culture* as in museums and opera. Rather, we mean the general tone and structure of the organization, and its policies and procedures.

As a young person trying to move ahead, do your best to pick a company with a corporate culture that recognizes and rewards ideas, and is open to hearing those ideas. Look for clues about the corporate culture during your interview.

BOSS

A good boss is more than just someone who is nice. It is also important they have the skills and patience to help you succeed in your position, should you need it.

An ideal boss is one who is also a mentor. That is, someone who takes an interest in your success, advises you, and prepares you for the next level.

PROS AND CONS OF JOB HOPPING

So, now that you've landed your first permanent position, how long should you stay? Career counselors say it's important to stay at a job for at least two years, but Gen Xers, especially those who work in the Internet industry, tend to job-hop more than most.

The pros of job hopping are that you increase your chances of having a bigger salary when you jump from one job to another. You can also finagle increased responsibility and a better title faster by going from one job to another.

The cons are that employers don't like to hire job-hoppers. It indicates to them that you're not going to be stable or loyal to them. Companies aren't willing to invest in training somebody if they are not going to be there for the long haul.

Another con is that you never really get any good feedback about your own development. You won't be able to see yourself operating over time if you're jumping around. "It is hard to develop consistency and even more difficult to master your own profession," says Jaye Smith.

One way to get around employers' skepticism of job-hopping is to build skills that are highly transferable. That way, you may not be judged for taking a better offer or for moving into a new industry.

Presently, there is such a need for good talent that it is no longer a strike against you if you move around. What you want to do, though, is make sure you are developing and sharpening your skills as you are moving from job to job.

SETTING UP
A TELECOMMUTING GIG

We've all heard the stories of a cousin's co-worker who's working from home while still being on payroll at the office. Visions of working in your pajamas with the television on in the background flood your mind. Aaah, wouldn't it be nice to work from home. No boss to worry about. No petty office politics to consider. So, why do some lucky buzzards get to telecommute while others toil away in the salt mines? Probably, because they had the guts to ask.

"For most people, the easiest way to set that up is when the employer already knows you, meaning you already have a good track record with them. They see you as a competent employee. You have a record of good performance; you may have a record of raises and increases, and usually when somebody is a good performer, at least they have a solid base from which they are working to make that request," says Career Management Counselor Karen Metzger.

The current talent shortage is working in favor of people making that request. Companies are increasingly creating policies for telecommuting.

The employee only has to make a business case for why working from home will work well for the company.

If your boss isn't in favor of you telecommuting, consider switching to a department where the manager is more open to the arrangement. Before switching, however, weigh whether it is worth shifting into another department. Another approach is to suggest that you telecommute on a trial basis. After three to six months, your supervisor can review the situation.

> *"Telecommuting will be a growing trend of the 21st century because it is mutually beneficial,"* MTV's Maude Divittis says. *"It helps businesses with space allocations and it helps the workers to be more productive and motivated because they don't have commuting time. It's also becoming easier to telecommute when all you need is a computer hook up and the telephone."*

The first step is to ask if telecommuting is addressed in the company policy. Generally, an employer will say that it is considered on a situation-by-situation basis depending on the nature of the job.

If telecommuting is in the policy, the second step is to write a proposal. Key phrases to use are *increase in productivity* and *increase in job satisfaction.*

For example:

> *I am a valued, talented individual in this organization. Jasmin Inc.* (substitute your company name here) *has attracted my talent. Now in order to retain my talent, please assure that I am able to experience the job satisfaction that works for my lifestyle. One thing that is going to encourage me to stay is a telecommuting arrangement. Such an arrangement will provide*

an increase in productivity and an increase in my job satisfaction. Here are the things I've brought to the company: Here, you would list all of your accomplishments, reminding them of who you are and what you are able to do for the company.

Diann Witt advises costing out a telecommuting arrangement by providing a budget. "It all depends on what the person is doing, but that is really the bottom line for many companies," says Witt. "The employer wants to know: Am I going to lose productivity? Am I going to lose the amount of work that you do? How does that affect the bottom line?" So, if you address the monetary concerns, employers are more likely to consent.

If telecommuting is something that you absolutely need, you should talk about it in the interviewing process. Bring up questions such as, Is there a likelihood of telecommuting? If it is a creative position, tell the employer that you need time away from the office to create, to think, to talk out loud, or to scream.

Just as not everyone can fit into the mold of the cubicle role, not everyone has the discipline to work from home. Make sure you're doing it for business reasons. Ask yourself: "Do I have the diligence to work in a solitary environment?"

CHAPTER 4

BANKING:
THE BASICS
AND BEYOND

For many Gen Xers, our first exposure to the concept of personal finance begins with a savings account. If you still keep your money in a piggy bank or an old shoebox under the bed, this chapter is required reading. But even if you consider yourself a veteran of banking, there is a wealth of advice for even the most savvy among us.

TYPES OF ACCOUNTS

SAVINGS ACCOUNTS

A savings account is essentially a place to park your money and earn a small interest in the meantime (just a step up from the piggy bank or the shoebox). Most banks require that you keep a minimum balance, but that is often not more than $50.

CHECKING ACCOUNTS

A checking account lets you write checks (for paying bills) which are drawn from funds in your account. The interest you receive in a checking account (if any at all) is usually very small, so it is not a good idea to keep an unnecessarily large amount of money in your checking account. It is best to keep the bulk of your money in your savings account, for example, and transfer it as you need it. Some banks offer "free checking," but it is important to read the fine print and get all the details because there may be a number of hidden charges and fees making the service anything but free.

Every month, the bank will send you your canceled checks (checks that have been cashed). Some people like to hold on to them for proof of payment. You might want to use that old shoebox.

A GENERATION X STORY

When Sheila Lawler moved to a new town, she switched her account from the savings and loan, where she'd always banked, to a branch of one of the large national banks located just two blocks from her new apartment. At the time, it seemed like a good move since the bank was so close, and she was familiar with it from TV commercials. The sign in the window advertising "free checking" was also attractive.

Sheila found out the hard way that she was paying fees for not maintaining a minimum balance in her checking account. Had she read the fine print on the checking account application, she would also have discovered that she was allowed only 10 free checks per month. Sheila has now switched to a local savings bank and has since been saving about $30 a month in fees.

BALANCING YOUR CHECKBOOK

The first rule is to always make a note of any checks you write—that is, the check number, the date, to whom the check is made out, and the total amount. Also make a note of any other withdrawals, such as from debit cards, and keep track of any deposits or transfers.

When you receive your statement each month, compare your checkbook with the statement. This is the time to spot any mistakes—look for bank errors on items you've missed.

MONEY MARKET ACCOUNTS

Money Market Accounts (MMAs) offer a higher rate of interest than ordinary savings accounts, but they also require a larger minimum balance (usually around $1,000) and have certain restrictions on withdrawals. You can usually write a limited number of checks from your MMA.

If you subscribe to the idea that you should keep a stash of cash equal to three to six months' worth of expenses (in case you lose your job or can't work for some reason), then a Money Market Account is a good place to keep that reserve.

CERTIFICATES OF DEPOSIT

Certificates of Deposit (CDs) are the highest interest-bearing accounts you can put your money into, and still have the FDIC guarantee that your money is secure. CDs are a one-time, lump-sum investment. You can open up a CD with a term of a week or ten years. Typically, people will get three-month CDs, six-month CDs, one-year, three-year, or five-year CDs. The longer the term, the higher the interest rate. Minimum deposits can vary from $1,000 to $15,000.

MONEY MARKET FUNDS

Don't confuse these with Money Market Accounts. Money Market Funds are a type of mutual fund, and they are not FDIC insured. Nonetheless, they are relatively safe and pay interest rates that are comparable with those of CDs.

MODERN CONVENIENCES

AUTOMATIC TELLER MACHINES

"How did people survive without Automatic Teller Machines?" you may ask yourself. Well, somehow they did (just like they survived without cell phones). But it certainly is hard to imagine a world without ATMs or access to your money virtually anytime, anywhere. ATMs are great, but you need to be mindful of service charges (sometimes as much as $5 for a single transaction) that can eat away at your hard-earned savings. Use your own bank's ATMs whenever possible since most banks don't charge their customers for using in-network marchines.

DEBIT CARDS

A debit card can look like a credit card, and even carry a VISA® or MASTERCARD® logo. But the difference is that your purchases are deducted directly from your checking account. You can use a debit card at places that do not accept personal checks.

Online Banking

First ATMs, now online banking. We've come a long way from our parents' generation when standing on a long line at the bank was a necessary evil. Almost every transaction you can perform in person is now available over the Internet—and at your convenience, without leaving the comfort of your home. During any time of day or night, you can check account balances, transfer money between accounts, and apply for a loan (among other things). One of the nicest features of online banking is electronic bill paying. Think of the time and money you save versus traditional bill paying.

Essentially, you can bank online with your "bricks-and-mortar" bank, if they offer it, or you can use an Internet-only bank. The Internet-only banks have some obvious cost savings over their traditional counterparts. The Internet-only banks can pass these savings on to their customers in the form of lower fees and/or higher interest rates.

One of the major drawbacks of Internet-only banks is that, other than direct deposits, deposits must be mailed in.

Direct Deposit

Direct deposit is yet another way to avoid a trip to the bank. The way it works is that rather than getting an actual check on payday, your employer deposits the funds directly into your bank account. (You usually receive a stub or statement letting you know how much was deposited, along with the usual information on taxes and other deductions.) Direct deposit can save you time because you don't have to wait in line to deposit a check, and you don't have to wait three to five business days for a check to clear. With direct deposit, your money is often available the day it is deposited.

BEFORE CHOOSING A BANK

THE HOWS AND WHYS OF BANKS

It is important to understand how a bank operates. Not because you might one day own a bank or even just work for one, but because it will help you understand the dynamics of your own transactions. Essentially, a bank makes its money on interest. In the simplest of terms, you (and a bunch of other people) deposit money into a savings account. The bank lends out a certain amount of money, charging the borrower a certain interest rate. It then pays you (the depositor) a small part of that interest and keeps the rest for itself. Look at the posted rates in your bank. Notice how invariably the interest depositors receive is lower than the interest borrowers pay. The other way banks make money is on service fees. For example, some banks charge fees if your checking account falls below a certain amount and other banks charge fees for writing a number of checks beyond a set limit allowed each month.

NOT ALL BANKS ARE CREATED EQUAL

The tendency is to choose a bank based on its proximity to our jobs or homes. But not all banks are the same. A little research can save you a bundle in fees. Look into savings banks. Many savings banks offer free checking and lower fees than commercial banks. Unless you own your own business, you probably don't need a commercial bank. When selecting a bank, ask whether it's a savings or commercial bank.

CREDIT UNIONS

You may have family or friends who belong to a credit union. A credit union is a not-for-profit organization that offers its members services that are similar to those of a bank, but often pay higher interest rates on savings accounts, charge lower interest on loans, and lower fees for other services. Credit unions currently have more than 70,000,000 members. One of the drawbacks of credit unions is that most don't offer ATMs, so you must use bank ATMs and pay high fees to do so. You also don't get canceled checks as you do with banks. If these drawbacks don't bother you, it might be worthwhile investigating if you can join a credit union. Learn more from the Credit Union National Association (www.cuna.org). Before joining, ask if deposits are FDIC insured.

ANNUAL PERCENTAGE RATE vs. ANNUAL PERCENTAGE YIELD

The difference between annual percentage rate (APR) and annual percentage yield (APY) has to do with compounding. The more often your interest is compounded, the greater the yield. Interest that is compounded monthly will produce more money than interest that is compounded, say, quarterly. When shopping around for Certificates of Deposit, Money Market Accounts and the like, find out what the annual percentage yield is, as opposed to the annual percentage rate.

CHAPTER 5

INSURANCE

No one likes to think about insurance. No one enjoys paying for insurance, and you much less want to think about collecting on it, because that usually means that something bad has happened. But the truth is, insurance makes good financial sense. The best approach to take when it comes to insurance is an informed approach. Here's what you need to know.

LIFE INSURANCE

Life insurance is the insurance people least like to think about, so let's get it out of the way. Life insurance is there to provide for your family if you die and can no longer provide for them. If you are single and have no kids, you probably do not need life insurance. If you are married and/or you have kids, you'll want to have life insurance.

There are two basic types of life insurance. One is called cash value insurance, the other is term life insurance. Cash value insurance is a hybrid of an insurance policy with a savings account. Part of your premium payments goes into an interest-bearing account. You pay a certain number of years, and then you are done. The catch is that your premiums are quite high in comparison to term insurance.

The way term insurance works is that you pay an annual premium that provides your beneficiaries with a pre-determined amount of money should you die during the term. The premiums on term life insurance are much less than cash value insurance—sometimes 1/10 the price! Experts agree that while you are in your 20s and 30s you should opt for term life insurance over cash value insurance, unless you are extremely wealthy.

AUTO INSURANCE

Unless you are engaged in a hazardous occupation or a dangerous sport, driving a car is the most dangerous thing you do on a day-to-day basis. The number-one thing you can do to control your cost is drive defensively, and avoid accidents and violations.

> *"What we tend to forget is our legal exposure and the possibility of injuring yourself and other occupants in your car," says Dave Snyder, assistant general counsel with the American Insurance Association in Washington, D.C.*

The basic coverages are liability insurance, uninsured motorist coverage, collision coverage, and comprehensive coverage.

The state's mandatory automobile insurance is usually liability insurance, which covers the person who you run into for damage to their property or their body. The second type of insurance required in about half of the states is uninsured motorist coverage, which covers you if a motorist who doesn't have insurance runs into you. Your coverage pays your claim as though it were insuring the other vehicle.

If you got a loan on your car, your financing institution is going to require you to carry collision coverage, which repairs your car if you run into something or are hit. In addition, you are required to have comprehensive coverage, which covers your car if it's vandalized, stolen, or damaged by weather.

Beyond the minimums, it's very important as young people start to collect assets to carry more than the state's minimum for liability coverage. There are no firm recommendations, but generally you ought to think about buying $300,000 or $500,000 in liability coverage and then even purchasing what's called an umbrella liability policy, which will extend those liability limits up to $5,000,000 depending on what you buy.

The worst-case scenario of not having insurance is that if you injure the person in the other car, you can be sued with your future earnings attached and all your assets are at risk. "Everything that you've built up or plan to build up are potentially at risk if you're not carrying adequate auto insurance," says Snyder.

Full auto coverage can cost anywhere from $500 to $1,500. But the countrywide average for automobile insurance is about $800 a year.

It could be more for younger drivers. The rates drop dramatically at age 26, but the rates tend to be high in the 20- to 24-year-old range.

In addition to age, the make and model of your car will also affect your insurance cost. Ratings are available from the Insurance Institute for Highway Safety and car dealerships. Generally, if you drive a high performance vehicle, such as a sports car, your insurance rates are going to be higher.

AUTO INSURANCE TIPS

Motor vehicle crashes are the leading cause of death and serious injury for persons up to middle age. A split-second mistake can take your life, disable you, maim others, and claim everything for which you've worked your entire life. So, purchasing car insurance is worth a few minutes of your time. Here are a few tips:

1. *Drive carefully and do your best to avoid accidents, thefts, and traffic law violations.* Your own prior driving and other claims experience is one of the leading factors insurers use to determine how much you'll pay for auto insurance.

2. *Shop around.* You can buy car insurance from independent agents who represent many companies, agents who work for one company, 800 telephone numbers, and over the Internet. There is a surprising variation in premiums charged by insurers.

3. *Buy more coverage than state law requires.* While virtually every state mandates a minimum level of liability insurance, you should probably buy $300,000–$500,000. Also consider purchasing an "umbrella" liability policy that will take your liability coverage up to $1 million to $5 million.

4. *When purchasing a new or used car, obtain and use information on its insurance costs.* If you finance or lease a car, the lender will probably require you to buy insurance to cover the risk of damage to the car from collisions, theft, and nature. The price of the insurance to protect the car can vary significantly based on its make and model.

5. *Explore with the insurance agent or company all of the ways you can save money.* For example, not using

the car for commuting, deductibles that you can afford to pay if a claim occurs, and discounts for safety or antitheft equipment are generally available as options.

6. *Buy Medical Payments coverage if your health insurance is limited.* Some states, with no-fault insurance laws, require you to purchase medical payments and wage-loss coverage, others don't. In the non–no-fault states, consider optional Medical Payments coverage if you have poor health insurance. Car insurance is nobody's idea of a fun product. But if you need it, you may really need it. So, spend as much time buying and annually reviewing it, as you would watching a football game. Odds are surprisingly good that you'll be glad you did.

Source: Dave Snyder, American Insurance Association

Renter's Insurance

When 30-year-old Hilda moved into her own apartment, she was so happy to be out of a roommate situation that she didn't think about renter's insurance. The same year she got her own apartment, she also got a raise. The sales executive furnished her apartment complete with new stereo equipment and computer system. After a particularly raucous housewarming party, Hilda's apartment was burglarized. She still doesn't know whether it was a friend or stranger who robbed her, but she's had to replace every valuable with her own money because she didn't have renter's insurance.

Not only does renter's insurance provide broad expansive protection for the place in which you live, but any injuries incurred by others while they are on your premises are covered as well. With renter's insurance, you don't have to worry about stray wires tripping up a neighbor or visitor.

If a friend comes over and trips on a wire, you would never think your friend would sue you. But Eric Goldberg, assistant general council with the American Insurance Association, says it's better to be safe than sorry. "I suppose that many people don't think of that. I mean it's a lot like all other kinds of insurance. You think it's never going to be you and then you realize you need it when it's too late," says Goldberg.

Typical perils covered by a renter's policy include fire, falling objects, country wind, robbery, theft, and vandalism.

There are two kinds of coverage: actual cash value and replacement cost. The actual cash value to replace a secondhand couch might only be $50.00, but the replacement value to replace it with like kind and quality would be substantially higher.

"You need to explain to your agent which kind of coverage you want," says Goldberg. "It costs a little bit more for replacement cost coverage, but some people are under the false impression that if they have old stuff, it will be replaced with new stuff because actual cash value takes into consideration depreciation while replacement cost does not.

"It would be helpful to take a couple of snapshots, take a video of each room in the house, kind of run through your closets and other spaces and keep that tape or those pictures off the premises," continues Goldberg, "so that if it does come time for you to make a claim, you can look at that and refresh your memory about what kinds of possessions you had."

> *TIP*—It's always a good idea to videotape or photograph your valuables because you would have a hard time remembering everything that you owned if you had to make a claim because of fire.

The way to purchase renter's insurance is to call your auto insurance carrier or call an insurance agent from a company where you might have another policy.

HOMEOWNER'S INSURANCE

When you buy a home on credit, mortgagers require that you have adequate insurance. Before you close on a home, they will ask for proof of insurance.

Homeowner's insurance is similar to a renter's policy. It covers the structure itself, contents, and liability. Be sure to ask your insurance company whether it covers jewelry or if you'll be needing additional coverage.

"Generally actual cash value costs a little bit less than replacement cost, but you need to think about what the implications are if there is a loss," says Goldberg.

Some insurance companies handle claims better than others. Ask friends and family for referrals on how promptly the carrier pays claims because levels of service may vary from company to company.

HEALTH INSURANCE

If your employer doesn't provide health insurance coverage, get it on your own. Don't go without it. You may feel fit as a fiddle, but a prolonged (and costly) illness can catch anyone by surprise. At the very least, you should be covered for 80% of your medical and hospital bills.

DISABILITY INSURANCE

Disability insurance is frequently overlooked, but is nonetheless important. Like life insurance, you need disability insurance whether or not you have people who depend on your income. Benefits are paid during that period in which you are physically or mentally unable to work (say, due to an accident). If your company does not provide coverage as one of the benefits, look into getting it on your own.

BUYING INSURANCE

The Internet has made it easier to buy insurance, either direct from the insurance company or through an agent. On the web you'll find sites that compare premiums to help you find the best quotes for the coverage you want.

CHAPTER 6
INVESTING

TYPES OF INVESTMENTS

To many Gen Xers, the world of investing can seem scary and mysterious. To some of us, it might feel as though we don't know the first thing about investing. Not to worry. In this chapter learn about the different types of investments available, investment vehicles, and important concepts about investing. Knowing the basics will put you in a better position to make important decisions—decisions that can literally change your life.

FIXED INCOME INVESTMENTS

As the name implies, fixed income investments are those investments that offer a known, pre-established (fixed) rate of return. The amount of interest income to be made on these investments is known at the time of purchase. These include U.S. Government Securities, Municipal Bonds, and Corporate Bonds. The common thread among all of these is that they are loans you are making to either corporations or governments. The terms of the loan are all spelled out ahead of time. The rate of maturity for bonds is 10 years or longer from date of issuance; for notes, it's between 2 and 10 years from issuance; and for bills it's under one year. Most bonds pay interest every six months.

Bonds and other fixed income investments are a good investment for those who do not like to take risks with their money (risk averse), or who want to balance the risk of their stock portfolio. It is widely understood that when stocks are performing poorly, bonds tend to do well, and vice versa.

Generally speaking, bonds don't pay a great deal of interest, but that's the trade-off with an investment that is virtually risk-free. Many younger people prefer to keep most of their money in stocks because they present a potentially greater payoff, but it is wise to balance the risk of stocks with the safety of bonds. As you get older, and closer to retirement age, you should begin to shift the balance over to bonds.

Here's a good rule of thumb. Keep nearly all of your investments (say 90-100%) in stocks until 35. Between ages 35 and 45, keep just 60-70% in stocks. Between the ages of 45 and 60, you might start out with 50% in stocks, and gradually decrease your percentage to about 20% by the time you're 60 years old. When you are near or at retirement, that is not the time to play the stock market. It is time for fixed income investments. In retirement, avoid having more than 10% of your money in stocks.

Bonds are known for their safety. Remember, however, we are essentially discussing loans. Therefore, the level of risk is inversely proportional to the borrower's creditworthiness (credit rating). You can count on the Federal government, for instance, to make good on its debt. You cannot be so sure about a corporation with a low credit rating.

Also, watch out for bonds with a call feature. A call feature allows the borrower to pay off the principal ahead of time, thus eliminating a certain number of interest payments.

Corporate bonds often have call features, as well as other provisions that can make them tricky and risky for small investors. Further, they are usually made available only in large quantities, putting them out of reach for the small investor.

Treasury investments (Treasury notes, Treasury bills, and Treasury bonds), on the other hand, are as safe as it gets, and most are designed to appeal to small investors. All Treasury securities are available in $1,000 denominations. You can buy them directly from your nearest Federal Reserve Bank, or your local banker or broker (who will charge a small service fee). Also available from the U.S. Treasury are savings bonds. Savings bonds can be purchased in denominations as low as $5.

A Municipal Bond is a loan you are making to a municipality or other local government agency or authority. They function similar to Treasury investments. However, since they usually require investments of $5,000 or more, they are not among the best options for young investors with limited resources.

Other government debt instruments are available from the Federal National Mortgage Association (Fannie Mae), Federal Home Loan Mortgage Corporation (Freddie Mac), Student Loan Marketing Association (Sallie Mae), Government National Mortgage Association (Ginnie Mae) and others. Each has its own set of rules, regulations, perks and risks, so get full details before you invest.

A Certificate of Deposit (CD) is another way to protect your principal investment and earn a guaranteed rate of interest. CDs generally pay a slightly better rate than savings accounts or money market accounts. With the CD, however, you make a one-time deposit that earns a fixed rate of interest for a specified period of time (term). Terms range anywhere from three months to 10 years. Beware, however, there are substantial penalties if you withdraw your money before the term is over.

STOCKS

Whereas bonds are debt securities, stocks are equity securities. This means that when you own stock, you actually own a piece of the corporation. You participate in the company's profits, if any, in the form of dividends (if they opt to pay dividends). Further, the value of your investment rises and falls as the price of the stock fluctuates.

Volatility is the name of the game with stocks. Prices can rise sharply, and they can fall sharply (often with little warning). The potential risks and rewards are equally great. Unlike bonds, there are no promises, no guarantees.

Stocks are generally sold in lots of 100 shares, known as a "round lot." If you buy less than 100 shares, you pay an extra transfer fee. You can buy and sell stocks through a broker on one of the many organized exchanges (the largest and best known of which is the New York Stock Exchange) or you can trade "over the counter" through the National Association of Securities Dealers Automated Quotations (NASDAQ).

All stocks fit one of two broad categories—common and preferred. Both represent a unit of ownership, but preferred stock holds a prior claim over any earnings and also has a prior claim to assets in case of liquidation.

REAL ESTATE

Unlike stocks and bonds, perhaps, real estate is something most of us can relate to fairly easily. Many of our parents own a home, so we have a good idea of what real estate is all about. But the picture becomes fuzzy when we discuss real estate as an investment option. In many ways, the rules for investing in real estate can be trickier than stocks or bonds. The value of a particular property can vary greatly, given a number of factors. There are few indicators of how real estate is doing as a whole, since you can have regional variations. Property value can even vary from block to block.

The best advice on real estate is to buy a house or apartment (if you want and can afford one) as a *home*, first—that is, a place where you'd truly like to live—and as an investment, second. Keeping both of these perspectives in mind, every good real estate agent will tell you what matters most is: location, location, location.

Despite what you may hear on the infomercials, building a fortune on real estate is not as easy as it looks. As the landlord, you are responsible for maintaining heating and plumbing systems, among other things.

COLLECTIBLES AND ANTIQUES

The advice on collectibles and antiques as investments is similar to what we said about real estate. That is, if you want to buy an antique or a collectible for your own use and enjoyment, go ahead and do so. You might get lucky and it may increase in value, but you shouldn't count on it.

If, say, you inherited a valuable painting from your grandmother who survived World War II in Europe, the first thing to do is to get it appraised. Find a reputable appraiser who can provide you with a certificate of authenticity, especially if you're dealing with an estate, and you want the value to hold up in court.

On the other hand, if there is a certain antique you feel you must have, check auction records. This is what appraisers do. There is a fine arts database at www.Artnet.com and www.iCollector.com. You also want to check the reputation of the gallery before making a purchase. Artnet.com lists information on various galleries.

INVESTMENT VEHICLES

Stocks, bonds, and other investments may be purchased individually or as part of an investment vehicle such as mutual funds, variable annuities, or Real Estate Investment Trusts (REITs).

MUTUAL FUNDS

The way mutual funds work is this: When you invest in a mutual fund, you are joining a large number of other investors who are pooling their money together. This money is managed by an investment professional, the fund manager, who will make investments on behalf of the fund. The fund will usually own a large number of investments.

There are stock funds, bond funds, money market funds, and other types of mutual funds. The kind most people are familiar with are the stock funds. You can buy any of a great variety of stock fund types—blue chip funds, income funds, growth funds, growth and income funds, emerging markets funds, technology funds, etc. The list is nearly endless and includes a number of overseas funds. Each type of fund represents a different investment strategy and goal. The fund manager actively manages the investments, adding certain stocks (in the case of stock funds) and dropping others; all within the vision and strategy of the fund.

The share price of a mutual fund is based on the net value of the fund's assets divided by the number of shares outstanding. So, as the value of the assets go up, the price of the mutual fund goes up. As an investor, you make money by way of any dividends earned through the individual stocks, capital gains from the sale of individual securities, or if the value of the overall fund goes up.

One particular type of stock fund, *index funds*, are not actively managed. They simply hold stocks that represent the components of a particular index. An index is a measure or barometer of how the market is performing. The two most followed indexes are the Dow Jones Industrial Average, which consists of just 30 large stocks, and the S&P 500 (you guessed it, 500 large companies). If you own an index fund, the value of your investment goes up as the market goes up, and down as the market goes down.

While the temptation is to try to find a fund that will "beat the market" (meaning, provide a greater return than the overall market as measured by the indexes), the truth is over the last 20 years or so index funds have done better than most managed funds.

Generally speaking, the advantages of using mutual funds are diversification, low entry cost, professional management, and liquidity.

Since an individual fund consists of many assets, diversification is built-in. You can get started investing with as little as $50 a month, which provides low entry cost to the stock market. The fund manager provides professional management. Liquidity means mutual fund shares can be cashed out fairly quickly. You are not tied to a specific term as you might be with bonds.

In selecting a mutual fund, look for a no-load mutual fund with low management fees.

Load mutual funds charge a sales commission, usually about 5%. No-load mutual funds charge no commission. Both load and no-load have expense ratios, which are fees used to cover such things as administrative costs and management costs. Select a mutual fund with a low expense ratio.

Be sure to diversify. You don't want to buy five technology mutual funds, for instance. Select funds that are invested in different markets, different sectors, and different kinds of investments.

Another factor to consider is whether the fund's manager changed recently. If the manager has only been there for three months and you are looking at a five-year performance figure, it is really irrelevant because the same manager is no longer calling the shots. You don't know how the new fund manager will do unless he or she has managed a fund in the past. If you're unsure about the fund manager, call the fund to ask whether there has been management turnover. If the fund manager recently left to start new funds, you might as well just buy the new fund that he or she created.

There are several different sites where you can find information about mutual funds, including Maxfunds.com, Schwab.com, and Morningstar.com.

At Maxfunds.com, you can find data on all no-load equity mutual funds, even smaller and newer ones. The data includes performance in class for each fund, the expense ratio, size of the fund, and trading volume. They consolidate all that information into a rating system for people who don't really want to do too much analytical work. They give funds a green light, a red light, or a yellow, depending on performance, expense ratios, etc. The service is free and by registering you receive fund prospectuses.

VARIABLE ANNUITIES

Variable annuities are a kind of mutual fund with some specific characteristics. They are available from insurance companies, brokerage firms, and banks. They resemble other mutual funds in that you place a sum of money into your choice of funds, all of which consist of a variety of invest-ments. They work similar to an Individual Retirement Account in that your dividends and capital gains are not taxed until you withdraw the money. Further, with an annuity, the contract stipulates if you were to die, your heirs are guaranteed to receive at least the amount you put in.

The drawbacks of variable annuities include the fact that they typically perform worse than other mutual funds. They are also subject to high fees. It is possible that you may wind up paying more in fees than what you make in income.

REITs

Think of REITs (Real Estate Investment Trusts) as the mutual funds of real estate investing. Much the same way that mutual funds leverage the capital of many investors to purchase a large number of stocks or bonds, REITs function similarly to purchase mortgages and/or proper-ties. Shares in REITs are traded on the New York Stock Exchange and the NASDAQ. The advantages and disadvantages of REITs are many and their complexity is beyond the scope of this book.

THREE IMPORTANT CONCEPTS

MONEY BEGETS MONEY—THE MAGIC OF COMPOUND INTEREST

It's important to get started investing while you're young because of the power of compounding interest. Compounding is your interest earning interest. The earlier you start, the greater the effect of compounding.

As an example, if you put away $10 a week in a shoebox for a period of 20 years (earning no interest!), you'd have $10,200. That same $10 every week earning 12% interest yields over $43,000 through compounding.

More dramatically, look at Figure 6-1 demonstrating the power of compounding on an annual investment of $2,000 made at the beginning of every year.

Dollar Cost Averaging

Dollar cost averaging is an investment technique whereby you invest the same amount of money each month, regardless of fluctuations in price. The idea is that you smooth out the highs and lows over time, thus limiting your overall risk. You can even set things up so that the same amount is deducted from your bank account and deposited into your investment account every month.

Diversification

This is perhaps the single-most important piece of advice anyone can give you regarding investing: Be sure to diversify. It's like the adage: "Don't put all your eggs into one basket."

Diversification is the best way to protect against risk. You are in effect spreading your bets. What this means in practice is that on one level you should try to have more than just one type of investment. That is, try to have something other than just stocks, let's say. While you might want to have the vast majority in stocks (maybe 95%), you should also have some money in something else (perhaps bonds or real estate).

On another level, diversification means having a variety of investments within an investment class. The idea is that your portfolio should include a variety of stocks, not just one kind. You should minimize your risk by having a wide variety of investments. That's why mutual funds are a great way to invest.

Number of Years	Annual Rate of Return		
	6%	10%	12%
5	$ 11,950.64	$ 13,431.22	$ 14,230.38
10	$ 27,943.29	$ 35,062.33	$ 39,309.17
15	$ 49.345.06	$ 69,899.46	$ 83,506.56
20	$ 77,985.45	$126,005.00	$161,397.47
25	$116,312.77	$216,363.53	$298,667.87

Source: Reprinted by permission of T. Rowe Price.

FIGURE 6–1   The Power of Compounding
Value of a $2,000 Annual Investment Made at the Beginning
of Every Year (Years 1–25)

A WORD ABOUT TECHNOLOGY STOCKS

As Gen Xers, we are known for putting a lot of faith in technology stocks. It may have to do with the fact that we've grown up with technology. But, as the market has shown recently, we need to be very careful about plunging into this very volatile sector.

"It goes back to the issue of diversification. It doesn't mean that you shouldn't have any technology stocks. We own technology stocks. It's just that I see a lot of young investors get enamored with one or two companies or one fund that is very concentrated in Internet stocks and they put an enormous percentage of their disposable dollars in those kinds of securities," says Larry Tabak, vice president at Mosaic Funds.

When asked if they agreed with the statement that the Internet companies of today will be the largest U.S. companies of tomorrow, 66% of Gen Xers said they agree vs. just 54% of baby boomers. (See Figure 6-2.)

The Internet or "dot-com" companies of today will be the largest U.S. companies of tomorrow.

	AGREE	DISAGREE
TOTAL	59%	32%
GENERATION (AGE):		
Adult Millennial (18 to 23)	78	20
Generation X (24 to 35)	66	39
Baby Boom (36 to 54)	54	40
Swing (55 to 67)	57	32
GI/WWII (68+)	45	27

Source: Scudder Kemper Investments

FIGURE 6–2   The Future of Internet Firms.

Generally, it's reasonable to put 10% or 20% of your money into speculative investments such as high-tech stocks. But to put 80% of your dollars in something speculative is not a very wise course of action.

GETTING HELP

Of all the generations, ours is the least likey to turn to a financial planner for help.

The fact that you are reading this book and this chapter suggests you are serious about your finances and investing, and getting assistance may be wise.

People who can help you invest have designations such as certified financial planner (CFP), chartered financial consultant (CHFC), or certified public accountant personal financial specialist (CPA PFS). Or, they may be brokers or registered investment advisors.

Like everything else, the best way to find a competent financial professional is through referrals from trusted friends. You can also call the CFP Board of Standards at 1-800-CFP-Mark to receive referrals of professionals who have a CFP designation. Interview the person before giving them your money.

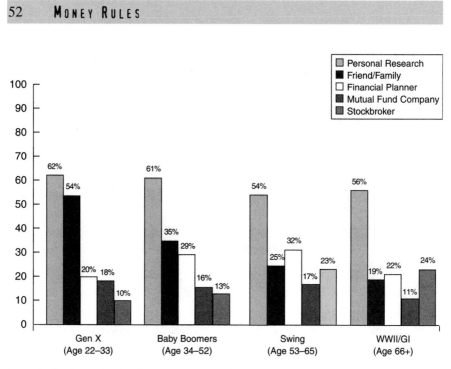

Source: Scudder Kemper Investments

FIGURE 6–3   Who Do You Rely on for Financial Advice

During your interview ask them the following open-ended questions:

- **What services do you offer?**
- **What is your area of expertise?**
- **How long have you been in business?**
- **Will you tell me about some of your clients?**
- **Do you have a sample financial plan I can read?**
- **Can you give the phone numbers of a couple of your clients?**

When hiring a financial planner, bear in mind the difference between commission-based planners and fee-only planners. Commission-based planners earn a percentage of everything you invest in through them, while fee-only plan-ners charge you a flat fee for their services and may also base their fee on the percentage of assets under management. As you can imagine, a fee-only planner has no vested interest in your investments, so they are going to be more objec-tive. Go with the fee-based planner.

While your planner is there to help you, always remember he or she is no substitute for having your own vision of where you'd like to be finan-cially, and how you'd like to get there. The "how you'd like to get there" part will depend greatly on your tolerance for risk. Appendix A of this book, Risk Tolerance Profile, will help you.

CHAPTER 7

INVESTMENT STRATEGIES

INVESTING IS A LOT LIKE EXERCISE: IT'S HARD TO GET GOING IN THE beginning, but it becomes easier once you get into a routine. There are strategies to make investing easier. They include dollar cost averaging, value averaging, indexing, and exchange traded funds.

MORE ON DOLLAR COST AVERAGING

Dollar cost averaging is the process of investing a set amount in regular intervals into an investment account.

The method makes it easy to invest regularly because it sets a schedule making it very much like getting up in the morning and going to work.

"People decide ahead of time to put some prefixed amount each month on a particular date no matter where the market is going, no matter how they feel about investments and that creates a discipline," says Meir Statman, professor of finance at Santa Clara University.

Your investment might be $100 a month or $1,000 every two weeks. Whatever it is, you are spending a fixed amount of dollars.

"In effect, it causes you to buy more when the market drops and buy less when the market is rising," says Scott Greenbaum, a certified financial planner.

It is a monthly investment plan but you can do it quarterly, annually, semi-annually, bimonthly, or even every day if you choose. Whether it's advantageous to do it monthly rather than quarterly or weekly depends on the person's cash flow.

"If you get paid on a monthly basis, it is easier to dollar cost average monthly. If you are paid biweekly, it might make it easier to do it biweekly," says Statman.

PAYROLL DEDUCTION PLANS

The easiest way to dollar cost average is to use a payroll deduction plan through your employer or to have a mutual fund company deduct money directly from your checking account.

> *"The payroll deduction feature causes you to pay yourself before you have access to the money to spend," says Greenbaum. "It gives you an added level of self-control in that you are paying yourself and not relying on monies to be left over that you think you want to invest."*

You must decide on the amount of money you can live without, then you acclimate your spending habits to having that much less a month.

With payroll deduction plans, there's no danger of forgetting to send in the money or of "chickening out" if the market falls.

VALUE AVERAGING

Another investing strategy similar to dollar cost averaging is value averaging.

Value averaging requires spreadsheets because it tends to be more active than dollar cost averaging and causes you to buy more shares when the market drops.

The difference between the two systems is that with value averaging, you plan for your account to be worth a certain amount at the end of the time period. In other words, you are investing to reach a preordained value at different time intervals.

For example, if you want the account to be worth $1,000 at the end of the month and the first month you invest $1,000, if the value increases higher than $2,000, value averaging would require you to sell securities to get it down to the $2,000 value.

The downside is that you would be paying taxes on the securities you sell, which makes dollar cost averaging more tax efficient. Value averaging is for the more advanced investor.

INDEX FUNDS

The advantage of index funds is that they offer broad diversification.

When you buy an S&P 500 index fund, you are buying the 500 stocks in that index in the exact weighting that they exist in the index. So, if Cisco stock is the biggest piece of the index, Cisco will be the biggest piece of your portfolio.

Mutual fund families such as Fidelity, Vanguard, State Street, Invesco, and Fleet all have their own form of index funds. Typically, you will find them based on the S&P 500, but you can get them based on the Russell 1,000 Indices as well as other indexes.

"An index fund is probably the broadest diversification bang for the buck. You literally get 500 names in your portfolio with one transaction, and it automatically adjusts as names move in and out of the index," says George Kiriakos, vice president with the Segal Company. "The index fund manager will substitute the new names and lose the old names from your portfolio. They are rebalanced typically monthly so that you are always pretty much in lock step with what the index is doing."

The downside to index funds is that when the index heads south, your portfolio goes down with it.

An index fund manager is considered passive because he or she only follows the weighting of the index, whereas an active fund manager chooses stocks and can trade in and out and is not restricted to an index.

So, if you are in an index fund and the S&P drops 20%, your portfolio drops 20%. If you have an active manager and the S&P drops 20%, you may only be down 10% or 15% because an active manager can trade in and out of losing stocks.

BENEFITS OF INDEX FUNDS

Your retirement account will probably not be the only source of money. Given the limitations on 401(k) contributions and IRA contributions, you will need to save additional money outside of your retirement account in order to get the kind of portfolio size that is going to generate the income you'll want and need in retirement.

Index funds are particularly appealing because fund managers don't sell stocks as frequently as active managers do. They don't turnover the portfolio's composition as often as actively managed funds. As a result, index funds don't generate a lot of taxable distribution year after year. You may want to invest in index funds within taxable accounts rather than in a tax-sheltered retirement account because index funds won't generate a lot of capital gains within your taxable account.

"In taxable accounts that you earmark for retirement, index funds make a lot of sense. For example, large-cap index funds are good. The case for indexing, I think, is weaker in small cap and international," says Mark Riepe, vice president with Schwab Investment Research.

RETIREMENT STRATEGIES USING INDEX FUNDS

One strategy using index funds involves investing a portion of each asset allocation in its respective index funds.

The idea is that you index 80% of your large-cap exposure, 40% of your small cap, and 30% of international. For example, if you're investing in large-cap stocks, then 80% of your large-cap exposure can be in an S&P 500 index fund.

"Index less in small cap, about 40%, and index even less in international, about 30%. If you adopt those percentages and use those three index funds as kind of a core of your equity portfolio, you are in pretty good shape," says Riepe, who advocates Schwab's Core and Explore strategy. "What you can then do is explore a little bit or take a little bit more risk by pursuing active managed strategies with the non-core portion of your portfolio."

FICTIONAL EXAMPLE

Mary Alsten has $100,000 to invest for retirement. Following the core and explore strategy, the mother of two put $40,000 (80% of $50,000) in large-cap index funds and $10,000 (20% of $50,000) in large-cap active funds. Alsten decided that she wanted $30,000 of the $100,000 in small-cap funds. She split it into two pieces and invested $12,000 in a small-cap index (40% of $30,000) and $18,000 in small-cap active funds. With the $20,000 leftover, she put $6,000 in an international index fund (30% of $20,000) and the rest in an actively-managed international fund.

"Core and explore is really a way of dividing up that equity portion to make sure that you don't get hit with any sort of big negative surprises due to an active management style that goes out of favor or an active manager who kind of loses his touch and ends up underperforming for a number of years," says Riepe. "It's protection in the form of that index fund."

Another strategy using index funds is to use the index fund to fill the large-cap piece of your diversification puzzle. Aside from that, you would look for a mutual fund that focuses on large-cap value, large-cap growth, and small-cap funds. "You can break it down into thirds and invest 30% in an index fund to hold down the middle of the road and invest 30% in active managers on the value side of that and 30% on the growth side of that. It has turned out to be a rather effective strategy for quite a few of my clients," says Kiriakos.

EXCHANGE TRADED FUNDS

Another retirement strategy is using exchange traded funds to accumulate money. Exchange Traded Funds (ETF) are like index funds, but they are traded as stocks. It is a basket of securities that trades on a stock exchange. Among the firms that issue ETFs are Merrill Lynch, State Street, and Barclays. Barclays ETFs are called iShares.

The two basic strategies, buy and hold or actively managed, are both useful in building capital appreciation.

The first strategy of buying and holding is passive. The second way to use them is in an active management scenario in which a financial advisor adjusts your exposure to different markets, different indices, and different sectors just as they might adjust stocks in your portfolio.

"It is a great strategy in preparing for retirement and, then once somebody is retired, it is a great strategy to continue investing for capital appreciation and generation of cash flow," says Jim Kelly, chairman of Addison Capital Management.

USING EXCHANGE TRADED FUNDS
AS A RETIREMENT STRATEGY

In using ETFs, decide how much money you will allocate to stocks in the equity market. The next step is determining how much you want in a core investment strategy, which exchange traded funds represent.

So, for example, if you want 70% in equities, you may want to put 30% in exchange traded funds and divide the remaining money into international, growth, and value.

COST OF ETFS

ETFs differ from index funds in that you can buy one share (but, as with stocks, if you purchase fewer than 100 shares, you'll pay a higher transfer fee), whereas with an index fund you have to buy into the entire fund (which often have a minimum investment requirement). Shares of the index are sold individually with ETFs. You can buy one share of the Dow Jones, the S&P 500, the NASDAQ-100, the Midcap 400 exchange traded funds, or iShares for about $75 to $100. "They are priced mathematically as a percentage of the index that each ETF represents. If the Dow Jones is about 11,000 right now, then a Dow Jones ETF is going to be about $110.00 a share," says Kelly.

You would also pay a commission to the broker because ETFs are only sold through brokerages, unless purchased in a managed account program with a financial advisory firm.

INDEX FUNDS VS. EXCHANGE TRADED FUNDS

The main advantages of ETFs are tax efficiency, accessibility, and pricing because ETFs are priced every minute the market is open during the day, whereas a mutual fund is only priced once at the end of the day.

An index fund may have an international expense ratio around 18 basis points, but an ETF built around the same index would have between 9-1/2 to 12 basis points at the current expense ratios being published by organizations that have sponsored these shares. For example, total annual operating expenses for the Vanguard 500 Trust is 18, for the Scudder S&P 500 index fund it's 40, compared with 12 for the SPDR ETF, according to Barclays.

Another advantage of ETFs is that you have a low entry cost; the downside, however, is you pay a commission to purchase them. There is no sales charge and no redemption fee with an index fund.

"If you put $1,000 into ETFs, maybe only $950 of it is getting invested. The other $50 is used for commission. You would have to invest $1,030 to have a net $1,000 invested in the Exchange Traded Fund from day one, but then your internal expenses are lower in the fund," says Kelly.

Chapter 8

Individual Retirement Accounts

Hello, IRA . . . Nice to Meet You!

An Individual Retirement Account (IRA) is a tax-deferred way of saving for retirement with certain benefits and constraints established by the government. The general rule is that you can put away up to $2,000 (under current guidelines) within any number of financial instruments, stocks, bonds, etc.

Just to give you an idea of how quickly $2,000 a year can add up: If you open up an IRA at age 25 and save until you're 65, you'll have more than $1.7 million, assuming 12% interest. Makes you want to run out and open up an IRA, doesn't it?

TRADITIONAL VS. ROTH

The types of IRAs available are the Traditional IRA, which can be a deductible IRA or a non-deductible IRA, and the Roth IRA. Because the non-deductible traditional IRA has no special benefits other than being tax-deferred, we'll limit our discussion of traditional IRAs to the deductible variety.

The two key differences between the deductible traditional IRA and the Roth IRA are as follows:

1. **You can deduct your contributions to a traditional IRA on your income tax; you cannot deduct your contributions to a Roth IRA.**

2. **Contributions and earnings are not taxed when withdrawn from a Roth IRA (at age 59-1/2) if you've had it for at least five years. They are taxed at the time of withdrawal from a traditional IRA.**

Other distinguishing features of the Roth IRA are that you can open a Roth IRA even if you are participating in an employer-sponsored retirement plan, and you can continue to contribute past age 70-1/2. As you can see, each type of IRA has it benefits.

QUALIFYING FOR THE DEDUCTION ON A TRADITIONAL IRA

In order to take the full deduction on a traditional IRA, you must meet one of the following criteria (as of 2001): (1) neither you nor your spouse

	Roth IRA	Deductible IRA	Nondeductible IRA
Earnings Grow Tax-Deferred	Yes	Yes	Yes
Earnings Are Taxed Upon Withdrawal	No[1]	Yes	Yes
10% Penalty on Premature Withdrawals	Maybe[2]	Maybe[2]	Maybe[2]
Tax-Deductible Contributions	No	Yes[3]	No
Maximum Annual Contributions[4]	$2,000	$2,000	$2,000
Subject to Minimum Withdrawal Requirements After Age 70-1/2	No[5]	Yes	Yes
Contributions Allowed After Age 70-1/2	Yes	No	No

[1]Withdrawals from a Roth IRA after five years are not subject to income tax or the 10% premature withdrawal penalty if the individual is at least 59-1/2, dies, is disabled, or uses up to $10,000 of the money for first-time purchase of a home. Withdrawals after five years but before age 59-1/2 for college expenses are not subject to a 10% penalty tax but are taxed at ordinary tax rates. Withdrawals of contributions made at any time are not subject to income tax or a 10% early withdrawal penalty. Withdrawals of earnings before five years are subject to income tax and possibly the 10% penalty tax. Note: Single individuals with adjusted gross income above $110,000 and couples with AGI above $160,000 cannot contribute to a Roth IRA.

[2]Taxable distributions are not subject to the 10% early withdrawal penalty if the individual is 59-1/2, dead, disabled, or if taking equal periodic payments over his or her life expectancy for at least five years or until age 59-1/2, whichever comes later, or for college expenses, first-time home purchase up to $10,000, certain medical expenses, and certain other uses.

[3]Must meet certain income level. (See table on page 3.)

[4]Total annual contributions to all IRAs (other than Education IRAs) cannot exceed $2,000 for an individual or $4,000 for a married couple filing joint return.

[5]Minimum withdrawal requirements do not apply during the account owner's lifetime.

Source: T. Rowe Price Associates, Inc.

FIGURE 8–1   Types of IRAs

participates in a company-sponsored retirement plan such as a 401(k) or (2) you contributed to a company-sponsored retirement plan, but earned less than $33,000 if you are single, or $53,000 or less as a married couple filing jointly. You can still take a partial deduction if you contributed to a company-sponsored retirement plan and earned between $33-$43,000 as a single person or between $53-63,000 as a married couple filing jointly. Looking at it another way, your contribution is not deductible if you contributed to a company-sponsored plan and you made more than $43,000 as a single person, or more than $63,000 as a married couple filing jointly.

QUALIFYING FOR A ROTH IRA

You can contribute to a Roth IRA whether or not you are participating in a company-sponsored retirement plan. You can contribute the full amount (albeit on a non-deductible basis) if you are single and your adjusted gross income is less than $95,000, or if you are married and your adjusted gross income is less than $150,000. If you exceed these amounts, you can still make a contribution of less than $2,000 if your adjusted gross income is less than $110,000 as a single person and $160,000 as a married couple.

CONVERSIONS AND ROLLOVERS

If you currently have a traditional IRA and you're thinking of converting to a Roth IRA, here are some things to consider. Your adjusted gross income must be less than $100,000 and you'll have to pay taxes on previously deducted contributions, as well as earnings.

If you have a 401(k) and are leaving your employer, you can rollover the money into an IRA without paying taxes when you leave the company.

INVESTMENT POSSIBILITIES

An IRA can be a mutual fund account, a Certificate of Deposit (CD) account, stocks, bonds, or almost any other kind of investment. If you open a self-directed IRA with a brokerage firm, you can include stocks, bonds, futures, and treasuries. About the only things you can't put into an IRA are life insurance, art, and collectibles.

PENALTY FOR EARLY WITHDRAWAL

Note there is a 10% early withdrawal fee if you take the money out of a traditional IRA before age 59-1/2, though, here are a few exceptions. You can withdraw without a penalty if you are buying or rebuilding a home, paying for qualified higher education costs, you become disabled, you die, you leave or lose your job after age 55, for medical insurance if you are unemployed, and for a small number of other unusual circumstances. There is no penalty for withdrawing your contributions from a Roth IRA. If you withdraw the earnings, however, there is a penalty.

SO, WHAT ARE YOU WAITING FOR?

Remember, the sooner you start, the better. Consider the examples of the early starter vs. the late starter below.

Given the benefits of an IRA, the best time to set up an account is right away. If it is before April 15, you can make contributions for the current year as well as the previous year.

FIGURE 8-2   Compounding Benefits of Saving Early

Year	Age	Annual Savings	Amount Accumulated		Age	Annual Savings	Amount Accumulated
1	19	$2,000	$ 2,240		19		
2	20	$2,000	$ 4,749		20		
3	21	$2,000	$ 7,559		21		
4	22	$2,000	$ 10,706		22		
5	23	$2,000	$ 14,230		23		
6	24	$2,000	$ 18,178		24		
7	25	$2,000	$ 22,599		25		
8	26	$2,000	$ 27,551		26		
9	27		$ 30,857		27	$2,000	$ 2,240
10	28		$ 34,560		28	$2,000	$ 4,749
11	29		$ 38,708		29	$2,000	$ 7,559
12	30		$ 43,353		30	$2,000	$ 10,706
13	31		$ 48,555		31	$2,000	$ 14,230
14	32		$ 54,381		32	$2,000	$ 18,178
15	33		$ 60,907		33	$2,000	$ 22,599
16	34		$ 68,216		34	$2,000	$ 27,551
17	35		$ 76,402		35	$2,000	$ 33,097
18	36		$ 85,570		36	$2,000	$ 39,309
19	37		$ 95,839		37	$2,000	$ 46,266
20	38		$ 107,339		38	$2,000	$ 54,058
21	39		$ 120,220		39	$2,000	$ 62,785
22	40		$ 134,646		40	$2,000	$ 72,559
23	41		$ 150,804		41	$2,000	$ 83,507
24	42		$ 168,900		42	$2,000	$ 95,767

68

Age	Value
25	$ 189,168
26	$ 211,869
27	$ 237,293
28	$ 265,768
29	$ 297,660
30	$ 333,379
31	$ 373,385
32	$ 418,191
33	$ 468,374
34	$ 524,579
35	$ 587,528
36	$ 658,032
37	$ 736,996
38	$ 825,435
39	$ 924,487
40	$1,035,426
41	$1,159,677
42	$1,298,838
43	$1,454,699
44	$1,629,263
45	$1,824,774
46	$2,043,747
47	$2,288,997

Total Amount Invested $ 16,000
Ending Value at Age 65 $2,288,997

Age	Amount	Value
43	$2,000	$ 109,499
44	$2,000	$ 124,879
45	$2,000	$ 142,105
46	$2,000	$ 161,397
47	$2,000	$ 183,005
48	$2,000	$ 207,206
49	$2,000	$ 234,310
50	$2,000	$ 264,668
51	$2,000	$ 298,668
52	$2,000	$ 336,748
53	$2,000	$ 379,398
54	$2,000	$ 427,166
55	$2,000	$ 480,665
56	$2,000	$ 540,585
57	$2,000	$ 607,695
58	$2,000	$ 682,859
59	$2,000	$ 767,042
60	$2,000	$ 861,327
61	$2,000	$ 966,926
62	$2,000	$1,085,197
63	$2,000	$1,217,661
64	$2,000	$1,366,020
65	$2,000	$1,532,183

Total Amount Invested $ 78,000
Ending Value at Age 65 $1,532,183

Assuming 12% annual rate of return
Assuming $2,000 IRA contribution made on January 2 annually

The Early Starter vs. the Late Starter

Age	Cumulative Investments		Account Value	
	Early Starter*	Late Starter**	Early Starter*	Late Starter**
30	$ 2,000	0	$ 2,180	0
35	10,000	0	13,047	0
40	20,000	$ 2,000	33,121	$ 2,180
45		10,000	50,960	13,047
50	No	20,000	78,408	33,121
55	Further	30,000	120,641	64,007
60	Investments	40,000	185,621	111,529
65		50,000	285,601	184,648

*Assumes $2,000 invested at the beginning of the year from ages 30 to 39, compounded annually at 9%.
**Assumes $2,000 invested at the beginning of the year from ages 40 to 64, compounded annually at 9%.

Source: T. Rowe Price Associates

FIGURE 8–3   Harnessing Time in Retirement Investment

Chapter 9
Getting Clear on 401(k) Plans

The Benefits of 401(k) Plans

You're in your 20s and you just got your first real job. Your paycheck isn't as big as you dreamed, but it's more money in your pocket than you've ever had. Retirement is the furthest thing from your mind, but you keep hearing about the disappearance of Social Security at dinner parties. To top it off, the lady in personnel keeps thrusting these investing booklets at you and encouraging you to take your 401(k) investing seriously. But why should you be worried about a 401(k) plan? Heck, you're only in your 20s.

If this is the way you think, get your head out of the sand. Quick! If you don't save for your retirement, no one else will. And the sooner you get started, the better.

It wasn't always the case that employees took an active role in their retirement savings. Most of our parents didn't have to worry. Years ago, most large companies provided pension plans. It used to be, if you worked for a company for 30 years, you didn't have to worry about retirement funds.

But more recently, companies have decided that they can't afford to provide pensions.

The 401(k) plan was established in 1981. 401(k) refers to the section of the Internal Revenue Code that allows this kind of retirement planning tool. The 401(k) plan was conceived by a benefits consultant named Ted Benna who looked at the regulation and came up with the idea that was accepted by the IRS.

The 401(k) plan is an excellent retirement savings vehicle. You don't pay taxes on the money you contribute until you take the money out (usually at a lower tax rate), deposits come directly from your paycheck, which keeps you from spending it, funds can grow substantially—especially if they are invested in the stock market, and employers match your contribution, usually up to 6% of your salary.

Here's a simple example of how it works:

You decide to invest $50 dollars a month into your 401(k), which is deducted directly from your paycheck. The money goes into your account, into the investments you have chosen (you can usually pick among stocks, bonds, and other kinds of investments). Your company will usually match 50% of your contribution (some do more, some do less). So, add another $25 to your account. Plus, let's assume a 10% return (could be more or could be less, of course):

> You contribute $50 each month.
> Your company contributes $25 more.
> $75 a month times 12 months = $900 per year.
> Add 10% return: $90.
> Your total for the year is $990.

Now, if your company didn't match, you'd only have $660 (assuming the same 10% return).

Another nice feature of the 401(k) plan is that the employee has control over the investing. The key is to educate yourself about your investment choices so, be sure to read Chapter 6!

The 401(k) investor can invest according to his or her age. A young worker can invest for long-term growth while someone nearing retirement age can put the amount that will soon be needed into an investment option that will protect the principal in the short run, such as fixed income securities.

Here's how employees across all generations allocate their assets within their 401(k) plans.

People in their 20s and 30s usually allocate around 60% in stocks, whereas people in their 50s and 60s allocate around 45% in stocks.

FIGURE 9–1   401(k) Plan Asset Allocation

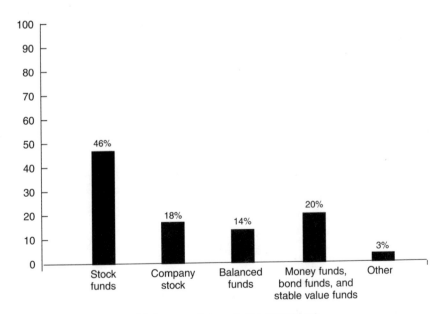

Source: Reprinted by permission of the Investment Company Institute (www.ici.org)

The 401(k) plan presents a terrific incentive to save for the golden years. Most people agree, they would not be saving as much for retirement if not for the 401(k) plan.

POTENTIAL 401(K) PITFALLS FOR GEN XERS

401(k) plans are terrific. But as Gen Xers, we have to be aware of a few potential pitfalls.

FIGURE 9–2   Would not save as much . . .

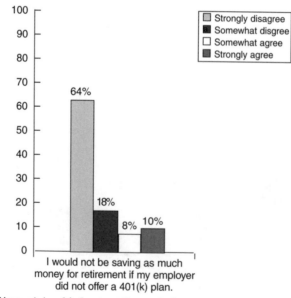

Source: Reprinted by permission of the Investment Company Institute (www.ici.org)

THE JOB-HOPPING PITFALL

Job-hopping is the norm especially in your 20s and 30s. Leaving jobs after 3 to 4 years can be advantageous in getting a higher salary, but it also has its pitfalls. The downside is that we often leave companies before being fully vested in the 401(k) plan.

There is usually a vesting schedule for any money the employer puts in a 401(k), and if the employee doesn't stay long enough to be vested in the company matching program, then we are leaving a portion of what was in our retirement account. Generally, you have to work 5 to 7 years to receive the company match fully.

DON'T CONTRIBUTE BEYOND YOUR MEANS

The average amount contributed to the 401(k) plan is 5% of your pay, according to Profit Sharing/401(k) Council of America.

Roger Smith, a certified financial planner in Sacramento, California recommends doing a careful analysis of what you can really afford to contribute. He suggests starting out cautiously, increasing the contribution slowly from quarter to quarter.

"Many young people jump in with both feet and contribute the maximum right away. They often don't have enough money to pay the bills and they end up using credit cards. This puts them on the slippery slope of high-interest debt. The key is to see how much your budget can absorb without hitting a wall," says Smith.

Another reason to stay within your means is that if you have to with-draw money prior to the retirement age of 59-1/2, you pay a 10% penalty and regular income tax on the money you withdraw.

Some employers will let you borrow from your 401(k). Repayments are deducted from your paycheck. This is a nice option to have, but it is always better if you keep your savings in tact. According to the Investment Company Institute, only 23% of 401(k) plan participants ever take a loan, where available.

If you can, invest the maximum in your 401(k), which is currently $10,500. That may seem like a lot of money, but increasing the amount you contribute on a monthly basis incrementally will make it a much easier bite to swallow. For example, you may want to contribute $200 in January, $250 in February, $300 in March and so on until you are contributing the maximum. Using this technique, you won't miss the money as much as you would if you put in a lump sum of $10,500. If you can't contribute the maximum, at least put in the amount of money that your company is matching. Remember the money your employer contributes is free money. If you think of it that way, you may be more motivated to put in the maximum!

FIGURE 9–3   Use of 401(k) Plan Loan Feature

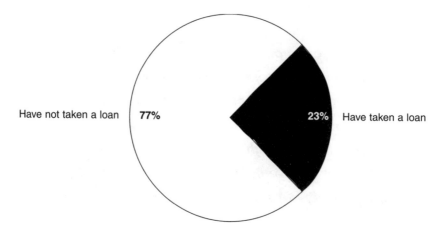

Have not taken a loan   **77%**   **23%** Have taken a loan

Source: Reprinted by permission of the Investment Company Institute (www.ici.org)

ON THE OTHER HAND, IF YOU CAN DO MORE...

If you are at a point financially that you can optimize contributions to your 401(k) without feeling too much of a pinch, consider putting away for retirement in other ways. Don't fall into the trap of investing only in your 401(k) if you can comfortably do more. As Figure 9-4 shows, most of us (67%) do invest outside of our 401(k) plans; but proportionally not as many as those belonging to the baby boom and swing generations.

BE SURE TO DIVERSIFY

While it is true that you have time on your side, and can therefore afford to invest in those stocks that have a greater perceived risk, but also greater potential return, it is nonetheless important to diversify. Don't, for instance, invest only in tech stocks. A good idea is to include international stocks, large cap, and small cap stocks in your 401(k) portfolio because they are usually on different cycles, meaning that one can be up and another can be down. Diversifying gives you a chance to lessen the bumps from putting all your money into one kind of stock. Also, don't go with just stocks. Consider other kinds of investments such as bonds.

Whatever investment types you choose, be sure of one thing: Begin contributing to your 401(k) right away.

FIGURE 9–4   Percentage Who Invest Outside of 401(k) Plan

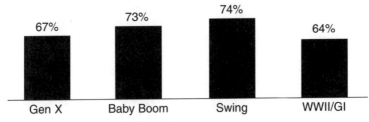

Source: Reprinted by permission of Scudder Kemper Investments

CHAPTER 10
GIVING TO CHARITIES AND VOLUNTEERING

THE GENERATION X ATTITUDE TOWARD GIVING

A GENERATION X STORY

Southerlyn Marino, a 26-year-old media executive, gives money on the New York subways whenever she runs into an entertaining act. "One time over Christmas, it was kind of a hectic day and I was on one of the busy trains coming out of Grand Central Station. People were looking depressed until these three guys started singing Christmas carols. It was so happy and fun that I gave them $2 or $3," says Marino.

Marino's parents were big donors when she was growing up and she says she feels that life has been generous to her. "It's the least I can do to give back to the universe in whatever way I can. I think whatever you give comes back to you eventually," she says. "It's good karma."

GENERATIONAL DIFFERENCES

Gen Xers give less than older generations because they are in the wealth accumulation part of their lives, which has to do with age and maturity.

"They will give and they will probably give to an even greater capacity as they grow older and their community citizenship expands. It really has to do with where they are in life cycle," says Vin Cipolla, CEO of HNW Digital, a digital solutions company, which focuses on the high net worth market including philanthropy.

In the meantime, volunteerism is very high among the young while the boomers are consumed with raising families or running businesses.

In middle age, there is not the level of volunteerism as there is with younger single people and obviously older people, who may be retired and have more time on their hands.

When married people in their 20s and 30s get involved in charity, they want it to be the kind of work that their kids, spouses, and extended families can participate in because they want to combine giving with parenting and family life.

"It's that balance they are looking for. They saw their fathers and their grandfathers spend those 50, 60, 70 hours a week at work. They don't want the same experience," says Sherry Abbott, director of the Philanthropy Center at Rollins College in Winter Park, Florida.

"What goes around comes around and if you are kind and good, the reward might not be necessarily what you think it is but it comes back in a very soulful way. It can come back in networking with a business opportunity or in simply making someone smile," said Mindy Kobrin, CEO of isupportcharity.org.

When people in their 20s and 30s give of their time, they want more hands-on involvement, such as delivering meals to the elderly or volunteering at a soup kitchen.

Young people are also more interested in events than in just writing a check because it helps them develop community with other donors. But the sort of events that Gen Xers are attracted to varies.

"Not all young donors like charity balls. It depends on the nature of the charity. Those [who] are attracted to environmental issues may be more attracted to hiking and walkathons as a way to raise money," say Cipolla. "Whatever the preference, getting together, community, that is all very important to this generation."

MAKING A COMMITMENT

A GENERATION X STORY

Natasha Strauss, a PR executive, sits on the junior board of directors of the New York City Inner-City Games and the junior advisory board of the Make a Wish Foundation in Manhattan.

The 26-year-old says that junior boards are put together specifically to target professionals under the age of 35 in order to groom the next leadership group and get young people involved early.

"There are lots of benefits to being on a board. You become part of a community, which is important if you live in an anonymous city such as New York," says Strauss. "It's a way to make connections and to feel like you are part of a larger community."

Some boards are very exclusive and require an invitation. Others carry a monetary responsibility of a minimum contribution per year.

"It's definitely a time commitment. For Make a Wish, we have a monthly meeting. For Inner-City Games, it's more quarterly and each one does a major benefit every year," says Strauss.

When Gen Xers get involved with a charity, they typically want to understand the dynamics of it and how it supports the community and how they can work with it. In other words, sending us an envelope and asking for a donation doesn't seem to work that well.

"They are very interested in the environment and diversity and inclusion. They are task-oriented kind of people and they work as a tribe. You have to get them all together for Habitat for Humanity to build a house. That's what they like to do," says Abbott.

People in their 20s and 30s are also more likely to volunteer for hands-on projects because many of them don't have the money to donate.

THE CHARITY CIRCUIT

A GENERATION X STORY

Ray Javdan, a 29-year-old Manhattan attorney, gives to the Whitney Museum, the Children's Hearing Institute, and the American Heart Association among many other charities.

But he's more likely to kill two birds with one stone by attending a charitable social event.

"If I'm going to an event, it's probably sort of a social event. For example, I was active with the Whitney Museum last year because they have a lot of events where you can see the exhibits ahead of the rest of the world," says Javdan. "I'm not someone who can spend 18 hours pouring over an exhibit, so I turn it into a social event by buying tickets to the Whitney Ball."

In addition to seeing the exhibit, the Westchester native meets with friends who are also on the charity benefit circuit.

"It makes it fun to take a friend who is in town or take a date and just enjoy something besides the usual business meeting or dinner and drinks with friends," says Javdan.

Paying for and attending a charity event also makes him feel that he's done something good.

"It's not one of those things that feels good where you have to question why it feels good. You can rest assured that it feels good because it is good," says Javdan. "But whether it affects you on a more deeper spiritual level depends on the individual."

Charity benefit balls are one way for hardworking Gen Xers to give or contribute while having fun.

Manhattan, Dallas, Atlanta, Miami, Chicago, Los Angeles, and San Francisco are cities in which people primarily work and succeed and advance themselves, which doesn't leave much free time for fun. Like-minded upwardly mobile young people in big cities flock to charity benefit events.

People have different reasons for attending an event. It could be because an illness struck a family member or strictly for tax benefits. For others it could be that it's a beautiful day in the park for a bike-a-thon.

TIPS FOR GIVING AND VOLUNTEERING

1. Organize a group of friends to volunteer for a weekend or participate in a charity sporting event.

2. Gather donations from friends to give to your favorite charity.

3. Find a soup kitchen or nursing home in your neighborhood where you can volunteer once or twice a month.

4. Involve your family in your volunteer activities.

5. Pick a charity that benefits you or someone you know.

6. Tithe 10% of your income to a church or charity of your choice.

CHAPTER 11
MONEY AND LOVE

DATING AND MONEY

THE TRADITION IS FOR MEN TO PAY FOR WOMEN DURING THE COURTSHIP period of an emerging relationship. But it is also true that whoever holds the financial reins tends to have the power in the relationship. So, ladies, if you want equal power and control, you may have to bite the bullet and pay your own way.

> *"Women want choices. By exerting or standing on their own two feet financially they maintain those choices. They maintain the power. Women are now much more used to having and using power,"* says Victoria Collins, a certified financial planner.

Rather than the man paying all the time, the woman might offer to pay every other date or, if he earns twice as much as she does, he might pick up the tab on the more expensive dates while she pays for less expensive dates. The balance should be in direct proportion to their incomes.

If you're the man and feel you're putting out too much cash, speak up. The woman may not know your financial limitations.

Whatever you decide in terms of money and dating, it's important to discuss financial issues as soon as the second or third date. Go ahead, pierce the veil of denial and taboo around money. The sooner you discuss it, the better.

GETTING SERIOUS: LOOKING FOR SIGNALS

As your relationship becomes more serious, it is important to know your partner's money style and how it compares with yours. Look for your potential partner's blind spots and weaknesses with money. That could be overspending, compulsive hoarding, avoiding dealing with money, excessive risk taking, and risk-aversion. For example, when you went shopping together, did she buy $500 worth of clothing on credit? Or did he use his debit card to get more money to gamble at the casino in Las Vegas? These are telltale signs of overspenders. He's a hoarder if he recycles sandwich bags and she's a hoarder if she uses coupons incessantly.

LIVING TOGETHER

If you are going to move in with a boyfriend or girlfriend, there are some financial DOs and DON'Ts to consider in the event of a dreaded break up. Remember, breaking up is painful enough. When assets are involved, it's even worse. The general rule is don't mix money until you're married, and even then you may want to keep separate accounts. If you do decide to merge your assets, discuss the financial issues before and during your live-in relationship.

A GENERATION X STORY

Reggie Greiner, 24, learned the hard way from his first live-in situation. When they broke up, he got all the furniture and she took $7,000—a lot more than what the furniture was worth. The second time around, the strategic development director sat down with his new girlfriend and laid out expenses on a month-to-month basis.

"We split them down the middle. Here's the rent, the utilities, the phone, all the way down to car service if we needed it. We don't concern ourselves with who did what during that course of the month. Expenses are just split straight down the middle," says Greiner.

Lesson learned. Talk about what you will do with money in the case of a break up before you move in so that you don't get the short end of the stick.

The best way to manage money when you're living with your sweetheart is to keep money separate. Set up a community account, into which each person contributes according to his or her income. From that account, plan on paying mutual expenses such as rent, utilities, and food. What that means is you have three kinds of checkbooks: yours, mine, and ours. In your individual accounts, called mine and yours, each person pays for personal maintenance, like hair, clothing, auto expenses, etc.

The amount of money that you contribute into the communal account is based on the amount of income that each person brings in. For example, if

Susie earns $250,000 and Tom makes $30,000, it's not fair for both to contribute equally. Instead, Tom may agree to pay certain expenses such as utilities, while Susie pays everything else. However, if Tom and Susie are both
making $100,000, it would be fair for each to contribute equally to the com-
munal expense pot.

> *"I believe if people are choosing not to get
> married, they are probably choosing not to commit
> deeply in lots of ways, and until they decide to
> commit, they probably should keep a certain
> amount of distance with their serious money," says
> Russell Hall, a certified financial planner.*

Even after marriage, some couples continue to keep separate accounts.
Hall says he knows of a married baby boomer couple who started living
together when they were in their 20s.

"They still don't tell each other what is in their personal accounts. They
have agreed it is off limits. That way, no one can get into an argument and
accuse the other of hoarding," Hall said. "I know a lot of married people who
keep separate checking accounts."

WHAT ABOUT DEBT AND RELATIONSHIPS?

In addition to emotional baggage, many Gen Xers have some kind of
financial baggage when entering a serious relationship. If you have no
debt and you're with someone who has a lot of debt, not to worry. You
are not going to be legally responsible if those debts were incurred prior
to marriage. You are protected legally.

So, debt shouldn't prevent you from diving into a relationship. But, what you want to find out before getting into a relationship is what kind of debt it is, the rationale for the debt, and how the person is handling it. It's one thing to have a $20,000 student loan for graduate school, but it's another thing to buy a $40,000 BMW on credit with the philosophy "credit is free money." That's a red flag. It's not only the amount of debt, the kind of debt, or why that debt is there, but it is how the person feels about using debt.

Why should you care, you ask yourself. Well, say, for example, you let someone use your credit cards. You get stuck paying the bills if he/she leaves. Go in with your eyes wide open, understand the situation, and if you are willing to accept it, then it's fine. To be safe, keep your credit cards separate. Never co-mingle them.

PRENUPTIAL AGREEMENTS

Whether or not to have a prenuptial agreement is a very personal decision. But, if you have a lot of assets to protect, you may want to draw up a prenup when you are living with someone whether or not you are sure you will marry that person. That's because in some states common law prevails. For example, in Alabama, if you live with someone for a certain period of time, you are judged to be married. So before moving in, find out whether your state adheres to common law marriage.

If you don't go to an attorney for a prenuptial, just type up an agreement you both sign. In this agreement, list all of the assets that you're bringing into the relationship. For example, list your computer, sleigh bed, washer and dryer, a condominium in Hilton Head, South Carolina, and other significant property. But, keep in mind, if you don't use a lawyer, there is a much higher possibility of breaking that agreement if it's challenged in court. Obviously, if neither one of you has any significant assets, a prenuptial will not be necessary.

Other financial issues to consider is whether you want your partner to be a beneficiary of your 401(k), other retirement account, your will, or life insurance policy in case of death.

PRACTICAL ADVICE ON SPLITTING UP

When you're in love, you don't want to think about the possibility of breaking up, but there are some practical matters you should consider, just in case. Say, for example, you buy furniture together and you break up three years later. You could just flip a coin with the winner getting first pick, but that doesn't seem fair. There is a more equitable way to ensure you don't get a bad deal. Each person buys furniture for one room. If and when the relationship ends, one person takes the bedroom furniture and the other takes the living room set. There's no mistaking who paid for what when you do it that way.

If you've already furnished your dwelling with expensive furniture together and you don't know how to split assets, you can hire an auctioneer to come to the home and apply auction values to every piece of furniture. Add up all the prices to get the total, divide it in half, and one person can pay off the other for his or her share. The same applies if one person is leaving and the other is staying in the house. Determine how much money should be given to the person who is leaving to compensate that person for what he or she is leaving behind.

Most couples can't negotiate until their thoughts and feelings have been aired and somehow lifted. You may want to consider divorce therapy. Even if you aren't married, it's therapy to give the relationship a respectful burial.

If it's a bad emotional break up where one of you feels abandoned, it may be best to meet again in three to six months to divide assets.

Chapter 12

Taming the Dragon of Debt

The Black Hole of Debt

About 5.4 million Generation Xers have an education loan, and 1.6 million have a secured line of credit, according to SRI Consulting, a leading market research firm. Further, 2.7 million Gen Xers owe between $10,000 and $19,000 in loans or credit lines, which is almost as much as their older boomer counterparts. This suggests Gen Xers are accumulating debt at a faster rate than Baby Boomers did when they were starting out.

The debts most Gen Xers face are student loans and credit cards. According to SRI, 79% of Gen Xers say they are concerned with debt. Consider the fact that 62% of us have credit card debt, and 49% of us say debt is an obstacle to saving for the future.

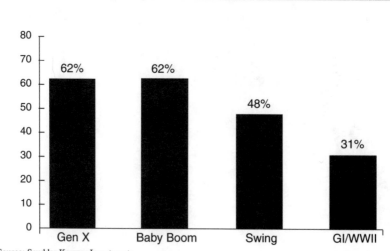

Source: Scudder Kemper Investments

FIGURE 12–1   Percent with Credit Card Debt

FIGURE 12–2   Debt Presents an Obstacle to Saving for the Future

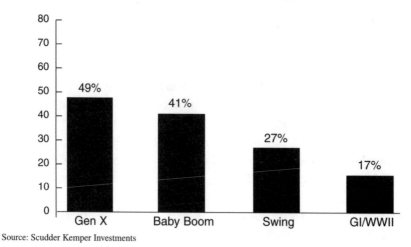

Source: Scudder Kemper Investments

HOW DO YOU KNOW YOU ARE HEADED FOR FINANCIAL TROUBLE?

The National Foundation for Credit Counseling (NFCC) offers the following questions:

1. **Are you unsure about how much you owe?**
2. **Do you skip some bills to pay others?**
3. **Do you have insufficient cash saved to see you through an emergency?**
4. **If you lost your job, would you have trouble paying for your basic living expenses?**
5. **Are you receiving calls from creditors about overdue bills?**
6. **Are you using an increasing percentage of your monthly income to pay off debts?**
7. **Can you only make the minimum payments on your credit cards?**

If you answered *yes* to three or more of these questions, you could be on the edge of financial disaster. Now is the time to take control of the situation. You must reduce your debt.

For sure, debt is not to be taken lightly. It can be a huge burden, putting a strain on individuals and their relationships. Money problems (including indebtedness) are often cited as one of the key factors leading to divorce.

REDUCING DEBT

To begin, calculate how much you bring home on a monthly basis. Then, calculate your monthly expenses. Make three categories of expenses: fixed, variable/fixed, and discretionary.

Your fixed expenses (items you need and the cost of which does not change from month to month) will include rent or mortgage, auto insurance, etc. Your variable/fixed expenses (those things you need, the cost of which can vary from month to month) include items such as food, utilities, and car repairs and maintenance. Your discretionary expenses (items you don't really need in order to live) include vacation, beauty care, charitable contributions, entertainment, and dining out.

The point of this exercise is to identify areas in which you can cut back so you can allocate the savings towards debt reduction. Clearly, the place to start is with discretionary expenses. You might find, for example, you don't need to have your nails done professionally every week or you can hold off on buying every CD or DVD you like. Make your own list of splurges you can cut back on or eliminate.

> *CAUTION.* It is important that you do not completely eliminate all your discretionary expenses. After all, these items represent those things you consider to be fun or make you feel good about yourself. You don't want to live a life that is void of fun. By leading a dull life, you might soon begin to resent your debt-reduction plan and abandon it all together.

The next place to look at for possible cost reductions is your variable/fixed expenses. Sure, you need to eat, but perhaps you can shop at a supermarket with lower prices or begin to use coupons. Similarly, you might look at your utility bills, especially your phone bill and cable bill, to see if you are signed up for the plan that makes the most economic sense for you.

FIGURE 12–3   How Do You Spend Your Money?

Are you satisfied with your ability to manage your income and expenses? Would you like to save more but can't seem to find the money? If you feel that a Cash Flow Analysis would help, please complete the following form using an average of your spending for the last 4 months.

A. *Fixed Expenses* (convert to monthly amount) Monthly Expenses _____

   Home Mortgage/Rent _____

   Other Mortgage_____

   Real Estate Taxes _____

   Maintenance Fees_____

   Auto Insurance _____ Homeowners Insurance _____

   Life Insurance _____

   Disability Insurances _____ Health Insurance _____

   Other Insurance _____

   Newspapers _____ Magazines_____

   Dues, Licenses, Fees, etc. _____

   Bank Loans _____ Other Loans _____

   Credit Cards _____

   Child Support/Dependents/Parent Support _____

   Savings Plan at Work _____

   Other_____

B. *Variable/Fixed Expenses*

   Food: Grocery _____ Meals out _____

   Heat _____

Gas, Electricity _____

Telephone _____

Water, Sewer & Garbage Collection _____

Laundry _____

House Help: Garden, Cleaning, Child Care _____

Clothing _____

Medical: Doctors _____ Drugs _____ Pet Care _____

Car: Gas & Oil _____ Tolls, Parking _____

Car: Repairs & Maintenance _____

Regular Personal Savings _____

Other _____

C. *Discretionary Expenses*

Entertainment _____

Vacation: Weekend _____ Annual _____

Education _____

Contributions _____

Recreation _____

Health Care, Beauty Care _____

Incidentals _____

Other _____

Other _____

Source: David Bennett, CFP

You are unlikely to find much, if any, savings in your fixed expenses, unless, for example, you decide to move into a cheaper dwelling or take on a roommate who can pay part of the rent and/or share some of the other expenses.

From those expenses you can reduce or eliminate, you've now identified a certain amount of money you will use each month to reduce your debt. So, what is your debt-reduction strategy? Apply the following techniques:

PAY OFF THE HIGHEST INTEREST RATE DEBT FIRST

Instead of making equal payments to all your debts, put an extra push behind your debt with the most astronomic rate of interest. Do this while you continue to make minimum payments (or more) on your other debts. If, your VISA card charges 18 percent interest and your Discover card charges 9 percent interest, put a greater amount toward the VISA. Once you've wiped out the debt on the highest rate debt, target the next highest rate item, and so on.

PAY MORE THAN THE MINIMUM PAYMENT WHEREVER POSSIBLE

A good rule of thumb is to round off the payment to the next $100. That is, if your minimum payment is $30, send in $100; if it is $120, send in $200, if possible. Not only will you be paying off your debts faster, but each time you look at your checkbook, it will also provide good visual reinforcement that you are making strides.

APPLY ANY EXTRA MONEY YOU GET TOWARD REDUCING YOUR DEBTS

If you receive cash gifts for the holidays, or receive a bonus at work, put it against your credit card bills or loans.

USE YOUR CREDIT CARD AS THOUGH IT WERE A CHARGE CARD

That is, pay off whatever you purchase in a given month on your VISA and MasterCard, the way you would your American Express.

IF ALL ELSE FAILS, STOP USING YOUR CREDIT CARDS

This may seem like a drastic measure, but for some it may be the only way to regain control of their indebtedness.

DEBT CONSOLIDATION

Debt consolidation is the process of taking out a loan or line of credit to pay off all of your debt at once. You make one payment to pay back the loan rather than writing checks to all of your different creditors. In addition to reducing the number of bills you pay each month, the real advantage is that you'll be paying a lower interest rate.

THREE WAYS TO CONSOLIDATE DEBT

1. You can transfer your debt onto a lower rate credit card.
2. If you own a home, you can take out a home equity loan.
3. You can go to a credit-counseling center.

Any of these methods can work, but you need to be aware of the differences as well as certain drawbacks associated with each option.

TRANSFER YOUR DEBT TO A LOWER RATE CREDIT CARD

You can consolidate onto one credit card, but the problem with that is the lower percentage rate may only be good for six months. If you can liquidate the debt within the time of the special financing deal, that's great, but most people cannot. The problem is that once the special deal expires, the percentage rate may jump up, so you really have to be careful before transferring your debt to another credit card. Read the terms of the agreement in small print on the back of the application to make sure it's not just a special deal.

A GENERATION X STORY

Tamara is a 23-year-old dance instructor. She wanted to transfer two credit card balances of $4,000 onto another credit card so she could make one monthly payment. The avid traveler got very excited when she saw an advertisement in the local paper for a credit card with only 4.9% interest. After she transferred the credit and actually got her first statement, she realized they were charging her 8.9% interest.

If Tamara had read the small print, she would have found the 4.9% interest was based on credit approval and a slew of other provisions.

Lesson learned. Look before you leap. Credit card companies often require a number of conditions to be met before you can get the "too-good-to-be-true" rate. Read the fine print before you sign up for any balance transfers.

HOME EQUITY LINE OF CREDIT

If you take out a home equity loan (assuming you own a home), the good thing is your payments are small because they are spread out over many years and the interest you pay is tax deductible.

"Frequently, the home equity loan is much less expensive in terms of the annual percentage rate they are charging you for the loan, and at the same time the interest is deductible from your income tax," says Matt Coffin, CEO of LowerMyBills.com, a website that offers home equity loans. "It is a bit foolish to continue to pay 20 percent on your credit cards when you could actually have a home equity loan at 8 percent, but on top of that the interest you pay for the home equity loan is tax deductible, whereas the interest you pay on your credit card is not."

The disadvantage is if you default, the creditor may take your house. Use the home equity loan only if you cut up all of your credit cards. "Treat credit cards from that point on as kind of like an alcoholic would view alcohol: as a poisonous thing. I have seen too many people who have gotten home equity lines of credit, clean out all of their credit cards to zero balances, and then go out and charged them up again, and then they didn't have any home equity to borrow against," says Coffin.

> **Home equity loans are great from a tax standpoint, but they can be very dangerous. "In the bankruptcy law, most states say you can't have your home taken away from you in a bankruptcy proceeding, but if there is a mortgage against it and you can't make your mortgage payment, then you can be foreclosed upon in spite of a bankruptcy," says Coffin.**

CREDIT-COUNSELING CENTERS

Let's say you had $20,000 in credit card bills. You haven't made payments in three months. You are supposed to be making a $1,000 payment. Your creditors are calling, saying, "Pay me, pay me, pay me." If you go to a credit-counseling center and work out a payment schedule, instead of $1,000 a month you may get it down to $500 a month—sometimes interest free.

> **"Essentially, you will make the payment to us and we will turn it over to your creditors," says Howard Dvorkin, president of Consolidated Credit Counseling Services. "We have national contracts with every major credit-card company. Depending on the contract, we will lower your payment by 30% to 50%, and reduce your interest pretty significantly or even abate it completely."**

Preventing Bankruptcy

Reducing your debts and consolidating your debts are the first steps in getting out of financial trouble. The measures outlined above will work for a great many people. For others, however, additional help is necessary. Consider these statistics: About 733,000 Gen Xers claimed bankruptcy in the past two years, according to SRI Consulting. In the next year, 425,000 Generation Xers are expected to claim bankruptcy.

The first step in preventing bankruptcy is to acknowledge you have a money problem. Second, assess how much you really are in debt. Third, get third-party help through a nonprofit credit-counseling center to come up with an aggressive repayment plan to repay your creditors.

"People with nine or ten creditors come in and sit down with our non-profit organization," says Dvorkin. "They can be counseled free or at a very low fee of $10-$20. We contact the creditors if they need that. We show ways they might be able to get out of debt without concession, because that can affect their credit rating."

Once you get control of your debt and have resumed making payments, it's all about changing your attitude from short-term gratification to long-term gratification. Now you may have to wait six months to buy the new stereo while you save the money, instead of immediately buying it on credit. In other words, you learn to live within your means.

A nonprofit credit-counseling organization can help you come up with a repayment plan and then follow it. Without a plan, people free up a few hundred dollars a month without dealing with the original problem. Then they fall into the trap of buying more on credit, and in effect, put themselves deeper in debt.

Be careful about selecting a credit-counseling center because some have outrageous fees. Choose a nonprofit credit-counseling organization. You can find a list of nonprofit organizations at the National Federation of Credit Counseling website, www.NFCC.org. You can also look in the Yellow Pages under credit counseling and then call to find out if they are nonprofit. Nonprofit consumer credit-counseling organizations are usually free because the credi-tors fund them. It is an advocacy organization, serving as a liaison between the debtor and the creditor, to negotiate reduced payments or forgiveness of certain portions of loans. However, these centers require consumers to stick to strict disciplines so the debtors have to take responsibility and get their finances in order. If all else fails, go to Debtors Anonymous, a 12-step fellowship fash-ioned after Alcoholics Anonymous for people who have trouble with money, or visit their web site at www.debtorsanonymous.org. If nothing else, you'll learn you're not alone and may find some relief while you're at it.

SO, WHY PREVENT BANKRUPTCY?

Until recently, it seemed all too easy to declare bankruptcy. We all know someone (or someone who knows someone) who has done so.

The fact is, bankruptcy is a serious matter. In effect, when you declare bankruptcy, you are making a legal declaration that you are unable to pay your debts. It carries with it the implication of failure—at least in terms of managing your finances. Further, all of the ramifications of bankruptcy are not widely known.

Many people aren't getting the full story when they go to a lawyer to file for bankruptcy. Many are led to believe there are no long-term effects. The truth is there are long-term consequences because the bankruptcy stays with you, not just for seven years, but in some ways for life.

For example, employers can pull credit reports on potential employees and you may not be able to get a job because of it. Bankruptcy could prevent you from getting a mortgage to buy a house. And, once you file bankruptcy, credit will no longer be extended to you. Stop yourself before you get to the point of bankruptcy. Cut up your credit cards so you are not tempted to buy on impulse.

"Under the new law, you won't be able to just walk away from your debt. You'll have to pay some of it back, if you have the means. It will be more difficult to claim bankruptcy," says Howard Dvorkin, president of Consolidated Credit Counseling Services.

A Generation X Story

Andy is $10,000 in debt for student loans that he has no intention of paying back. He took out a Pell Grant to pay for tuition at the Acting Conservatory in New York City. "In addition to taking the grant, you also had to take out a personal loan. I didn't know this. I've subsequently learned that my mother took out a $5,000 personal loan for herself on top of my grant. She's dead now, so the loans are all in my name and I'm stuck with a $10,000 debt from my mom taking out personal loans," says Andy.

He's counting on the myth that if you don't touch student loans for seven years, they go away. "I've just been running from it to tell you the truth. I heard the government eats it after seven years. This is the theory I heard from everybody. Everything was all going smoothly because I hadn't made payments in seven years. Then just three weeks ago I got a letter in the mail, they found me again."

Lesson learned. You can't run away from your debts.

As we go to press, the bankruptcy bill is awaiting a conference between the House and Senate. Once that's resolved, the bill will almost certainly pass. It takes effect 180 days after the president signs it into law. President Bush is expected to sign the bill by the end of 2001.

Here are some changes to expect as a result of the new law:

To prevent you from misstating what you earn, your disclosure of income and assets must now include your most recent tax return.

Mandatory consumer credit counseling, at your own expense, during which the counseling service will try to work out a repayment plan that satisfies your creditors.

If, after counseling, you can't repay, you'll file for bankruptcy. This action stops the clock on the late charges on your outstanding bills.

Exception: You can file automatically for Chapter 7 if you earn less than the median income in your state. (Chapter 7 bankruptcy allows you to erase unsecured debts—mainly credit card debts.)

THE SEVEN-YEAR MYTH

If you default on your debt, believing the slate will be clean in seven years, think again. There is a seven-year statute of limitations on the negative information staying on your credit report, but there are always circumstances in which the creditor can argue to keep it on longer. The same item could be on your credit report for 15 years. It's not a good idea to rely on that seven-year rule. If you have financial obligations, you need to fulfill them.

Further, the seven-year rule doesn't apply to all student loans. There is no statute of limitations for collection on student loans if it is a federal obligation. You will owe it for the rest of your life, and they will take it out of your tax refunds if they have to.

> *"They will get paid one way or another and it's scary. I have a client with a $6,000 student loan that turned into $26,000 fifteen years later because he didn't pay, and there is very little room for negotiation," says Dvorkin.*

REPAIRING CREDIT

If you've been running away from your debts and have decided to turn yourself in, or if you've simply messed up along the way, here's what to do to begin repairing your credit. Start by getting a copy of your credit report. You can get a copy from any of the major reporting agencies: Experian (www.experian.com), Equifax (www.equifax.com), and Transunion (www.transunion.com).

CLEAR UP ANY ERRORS

If you find information listed on your report that is inaccurate, gather the necessary documentation, such as canceled checks, settlement papers or legal papers, and forward copies to the credit reporting company. If you can't find the papers you need to prove the bill was paid or that the bill is not yours, the alternative would be to contact the creditor. For example, if it shows you have an outstanding medical bill from years ago, contact the hospital and request its billing department provide you with proof that you paid the debt.

CONTACT CREDITORS TO WHOM PAYMENTS ARE OVERDUE IN ORDER TO ESTABLISH GOOD FAITH AND A PAYMENT PLAN

Pick up the phone and let them know you would like to work out a plan. Most will work with you. Then it is important that you stick to that plan.

BE CURRENT IN YOUR PAYING CYCLE

This means, with old and new debts alike, when you get a bill, you pay it within the 30-day statement period. Sounds obvious, but it is essential to repairing your credit. The good news is that after about a year, when you have paid on time in good faith, credit begins to repair itself.

SUMMARY OF KEY POINTS

- We Gen Xers have a great deal of debt—somewhat disproportionate to other generations given our age—mostly from student loans and credit card bills.

- We can take certain measures to reduce debt, as well as consolidate debt. There are several options for consolidating, but it is important to understand the differences.

- If, after attempting debt reduction and debt consolidation techniques, you find you are still in financial trouble, it is time to seek help in order to prevent bankruptcy.

- Bankruptcy is not so benevolent as some would have you think. There are long-term consequences you may not know about.

- With some help, it is possible to turn around even the bleakest of financial situations. Repairing your credit is not impossible.

CHAPTER 13

31 WAYS
TO SAVE MONEY

IF THERE IS ONE THING THAT'S TRUE, IT'S THAT YOU ARE NEVER TOO young (or too old) to save money. You're also never too rich (or too poor) to save money. Saving money is for everyone. Here are a few creative ways to keep your expense down.

FOOD

AVOID PURCHASING AT A MINI-MART

OR CONVENIENCE STORE

You're paying for convenience at the convenience store. Don't make it a habit to get your groceries there. Most convenience stores and minimarts are too small to buy goods in large quantities (as would a super-market), so they can't take advantage of volume discounts (the way larger grocers do), and therefore prices tend to be high. Go to the supermarket or wholesale club.

BE AWARE OF PRICES WHEN YOU SHOP FOR GROCERIES

Many supermarkets make it easy to comparison shop by providing per-unit cost labels on their shelves. These labels allow you to compare the cost per pound, of one brand over another. You can also save by buying in larger quantities. And, of course, clip those coupons!

PACK A LUNCH INSTEAD OF EATING OUT

The cost of eating lunch out every day can really add up. It's really much less expensive to prepare your own lunch. The time it takes you to prepare your lunch in the morning is probably less than the time it takes you to get to the restaurant and be served. Not only will you save money this way, but you'll also have more free time at lunch—just don't use that time to go shopping!

THE "SPECIAL" AT A RESTAURANT DOESN'T MEAN IT'S ON SALE

Special items simply refer to items that may not be on the menu. Often, these items are more expensive than regular menu items. Always ask how much the "special" costs.

DON'T BE TOO PROUD TO ASK FOR

A DOGGIE BAG AT THE RESTAURANT

If you've decided to treat yourself to eating out (not exactly the best way to save money, but oh well), be sure to ask for a doggie bag if you have leftovers. Those leftovers could be tomorrow's lunch. By doing so, you've spread your eating-out expense over two meals.

Home

FIX LEAKY FAUCETS AND TOILETS

Whether or not you're paying for your water consumption (apartment renters usually don't, homeowners do), be sure not to waste water. Fix leaks right away.

WAIT UNTIL YOU HAVE A FULL LOAD BEFORE YOU

RUN THE DISHWASHER OR CLOTHES WASHER

These appliances are using not only water, but also electricity. The more efficiently you run them, the better.

AS BULBS BLOW OUT, TRY REPLACING THEM WITH

LOWER WATTAGE BULBS

If, for instance, you have 100-watt bulbs in your lamps, try using 75-watt bulbs. The only difference you may notice might be in your electric bill.

Find second-hand furniture
and get creative

Buy furniture from retirees who have downsized and are looking to get rid of stuff. Look for home sales in the newspaper or ask Mom and Dad about family and friends.

Look at the energy efficiency rating
on any new appliances you buy

Most appliances list an energy efficiency rating. Everything else being equal, buy those appliances (such as air conditioners, refrigerators, etc.) with the best energy efficiency.

Shopping

Avoid buying clothes that are
"dry clean only"

When you buy clothes that are dry clean only, you are getting a garment that is probably more expensive than those that can be washed at home, plus you're adding the expense of the perpetual dry cleaning.

Buy gifts off season
and when they are on sale

Think ahead. If you see something at discount in July that's appropriate for a gift in December, go ahead and buy it.

Buy insurance for your cell phone

If you lose it, you only have to pay a replacement fee.

Banking

Transfer your balance
to a low-interest credit card

If you have a balance on a high interest credit card, transfer that balance to a lower-rate card. Make sure that your card does not charge you an annual fee. If the low rate expires after a certain period, transfer again.

Start an automatic deposit savings account

Authorize an automatic transfer of $100 a month from your checking account to your savings account.

Be aware of the cost for those banking services extras

Don't use overdraft protection for your checking account. There is a daily interest rate that accrues if you don't pay the overdraft right away.

Internet

Switch to a free Internet service provider

There are a number of companies that now offer free Internet access. One of the most popular is NetZero (www.netzero.com). You can also get free e-mail on a number of sites, including Yahoo (www.yahoo.com).

GET FREE PHONE SERVICE OVER THE INTERNET

If you have an Internet connection, you can make free phone calls on your computer using a service such as Net2Phone. You can call anywhere in the U.S. for free.

FIND PHONE NUMBERS ON THE INTERNET INSTEAD OF 411

Directory assistance (411) is not a free service. Look up the number on the Internet instead at www.555-1212.com

LOOK FOR FREE SAMPLES ON THE INTERNET

Several sites offer free samples for a variety of consumer products. These are companies that want you to use or switch to their products. Some may be samples of products you already use. See www.freesamples.com, www.coolfreebielinks.com, and www.startsampling.com.

TRANSPORTATION

SWITCH FROM PREMIUM TO REGULAR GASOLINE

Most cars don't need premium gasoline (check your owner's manual to see what octane you need). Use regular instead; your car will run just fine.

KEEP YOUR TIRES INFLATED
TO THE RIGHT LEVEL

Keeping your tires inflated to the right level gets you better mileage.

CHANGE THE AIR FILTER IN YOUR CAR YOURSELF

You can buy the air filter at a discount store and easily replace it yourself, rather than pay a premium at a mechanic or lube shop.

CARPOOL

There are so many benefits to carpooling. First, you save money by using your car only a fraction of the time versus commuting alone. Second, you can speed through traffic faster at rush hour by taking advantage of the special "high occupancy vehicle" (HOV) lanes. Last, but certainly not least, you are reducing the number of cars on the road, therefore doing your share to reduce pollution and protect the environment.

TRAVEL

LOOK INTO INEXPENSIVE VACATION ALTERNATIVES

Going off to exotic lands can put a real dent into your savings. Consider vacationing close to home, perhaps somewhere you can get to by car in just a few hours. You might think about a camping trip, or simply spending a week seeing the sights you have close to home (including some free or low-cost museums and parks) while "lodging" at home.

Sign up with the Appalachian or Adirondack Mountain Club (www.outdoors.org) or Sierra club organizations that offer group hiking trips near lakes for $25 per weekend, including lodging, food, and transportation.

AVOID DUPLICATE INSURANCE COVERAGE WHEN RENTING A CAR

A number of credit card companies provide insurance coverage when you rent a car on their card. Don't get the same insurance from the rental company.

BOOK AIRLINE TRAVEL AT LEAST 21 DAYS IN ADVANCE AND INCLUDE A SATURDAY-NIGHT STAY OVER

You'll generally pay a premium for last-minute airline reservations. You also tend to pay more if you don't stay over on a Saturday night. If your plans are really flexible, try traveling on stand-by. Look into www.cheaptickets.com.

LEISURE

BORROW BOOKS, AUDIOTAPES, CDS, AND VIDEOS FROM THE LIBRARY

Most of us think of the library as a place to borrow books, but most public libraries also lend audiotapes (especially books on tape), compact discs, and videotapes—all for free! Depending on your local library, its collections can be extensive. Do return any items you borrow on time to avoid late charges.

TRY THE "Y" INSTEAD OF AN EXPENSIVE GYM

Your local YMCA/YWCA or YMJA/YWJA may provide exercise facilities that rival the neighborhood high-priced gym. Many even offer access to swimming pools, all for a fraction of the cost.

SPEND SOME TIME IN YOUR LOCAL PARK

Buy a bike or jog instead of joining a gym.

CHECK YOUR NEIGHBORHOOD NEWSPAPER FOR THINGS TO DO

Attend free arts and entertainment events in your city.

CHAPTER 14

AFFORDING YOUR VACATION

FINANCING A VACATION

THE TENDENCY FOR MANY IS TO PLAN ON PAYING FOR A VACATION USING their IRS tax refund. This is fine if you're absolutely sure you're getting a refund, and a substantial one at that! But, let's say you are planning a trip to Hawaii next summer. Your plan is to finance the trip with your tax refund. What happens if you don't get the refund you expected? If you've already booked your trip, you may find yourself stuck with the hotel and air reservations.

So, play it safe: Set up a special vacation savings account where you can save money to pay for your trip. When planning how much to save, don't forget to factor in money for added expenses, such as for snorkeling or scuba diving lessons if you are going to the ocean.

117

Realistically, if the year goes by and you haven't saved a dime, then you have to skip the vacation. But, keeping that in mind should keep you on your toes about depositing money in your special vacation account.

"You shouldn't take a vacation unless you already have the money. Don't charge it and then pay for it later. Pay for it before you take your vacation by saving ahead of time," says M. Eileen Dorsey, a certified financial planner.

If your trip (including incidentals) will cost you around $3,000, save $250-$300 a month the year before you take the trip. Keep yourself motivated by looking through travel brochures and checking the balance on your special savings account. Keep a picture of your destination on the outside of the refrigerator door.

There are some credit card programs that offer frequent flyer miles to help pay for your airline tickets. If you use one of these incentive programs to get a free ticket, that's less money you have to save monthly. But, be careful to not fall into the trap of buying on credit just for the bonus miles. Charge only those items you'll be paying off at the end of the month.

BE WARY OF TRAVEL PARTNERS

Traveling with someone else can present savings—by sharing the expense of a hotel room, for example—but beware. People can be the best friends in the world, but just like living with a roommate, traveling with someone else can change the relationship. During the course of your trip, you may not agree on the little things, like being on your feet and walking around all day. For example, this person walks too fast or too slow. Or, your best friend wants to talk to an attractive person at the Michelangelo statue in Italy, but you want to move on. Worse yet, your travel partner may snore, keeping you up at night.

Select a travel partner wisely because a bad choice could wreck your experience if you're not compatible. Find out if you and your partner like to do the same things. You may want to take a three-day mini-vacation to Lake

Tahoe or to the Berkshires to find out what kind of travel partner he or she is before committing to an extended vacation.

Package Trips Vs. Do-It-Yourself Planning

A package trip usually provides the airfare, accommodations, and a full itinerary. For example, if traveling to Europe, there would be a plan for your day in each city. There are other packages that might allow for more flexibility. For example, in Paris they reserve a hotel for you, but the rest of the sightseeing is up to you. Generally, you have to participate in the itinerary they've created for you.

The advantages of a package tour include, first, the social aspect since you'll be traveling with a group, and, second, you don't have to worry about planning. Other people take care of the itinerary for you. You don't have to worry about catching the plane or your next meal. Travelers like the concept of the package because it makes things easy and it gives them the one price they can relate to as far as being able to afford it. At www.contiki.com, you can find package trips designed specifically for those between the ages of 18 and 35.

The downside is that the package offers less freedom. That is, you generally can't customize package trips. For example, you can't say, "I like this 12-day tour of Greece, but I would like to stay 16 days instead of 12" or "I like these first 8 days, but I would like to change the last four days." Most tour operators aren't going to give you that flexibility.

If you do decide on a package tour, get referrals. "There is nothing worse than getting on a package tour and realizing the 15 others are people you don't get along with or the itinerary is not what you wanted," says Gregg Bleakney, CEO of www.Wherenext.com, a Gen X travel site where you can customize guidebooks and pick up discounts.

When you forego package trips and do it yourself instead, your experiences as an independent traveler are totally unique. It is something you can call your own. The downside is booking the tickets, the hotels, and the planning on your own. The good news is you can do that with the help of the Internet.

"It's important for the customer to get as much information as possible about the destination itself. Find out about the places you're going to be, the location of hotels, types of hotels, and how you'll get around," says Bernard Frelat, chairman and CEO of www.Eurovacations.com. This site suggests activities and attractions to see in various European cities.

Whether it's on the Internet or through guidebooks, be sure to do sufficient research so you can pick the right destination, at the right price.

RESORTS

Young professionals, who have the cash to spend and don't want to worry about anything, may want to consider resorts like Club Med. Such destinations as Cancun and the Turquoise Islands have become popular destinations, especially for long holiday weekends when the airlines and travel agencies offer discounts. They provide organized activities and it's all-inclusive. For a week, plan to spend anywhere between $1,000 and $1,500.

CHAPTER 15
BUYING A HOME

IF YOU ARE READING THIS CHAPTER, CHANCES ARE YOUR SITUATION COMES fairly close to Scenario 3 we described at the end of Chapter 1. That is, you are likely in your 30s, probably married, and perhaps you have a child or one on the way. You might find yourself in a two-bedroom apartment and feeling a bit cramped.

But whatever your circumstances, if you are a Gen Xer looking for your first home, there are a few things you need to know, and a few questions you need to ask yourself. Not the least of these questions is: How much home can you afford?

QUALIFYING FOR A MORTGAGE

Unless you are planning to pay for your home in full with cash (in which case, go ahead and skip this chapter), you'll need to qualify for a mortgage. A mortgage is a loan for the purchase of real estate where the collateral (what the lender would take if you were to default on the loan) is the property itself. Most mortgages require that you give the seller a down payment of anywhere between 3-20%. That's just the beginning. Lenders also want to look at your income to make sure that the principal, interest, real estate taxes, and homeowners insurance (together known as PITI) will not exceed 28% of your total monthly income. They'll also want to look at your other debts (in addition to the PITI) to see if all your monthly debt obligations (car loans, student loans, etc.) don't exceed 36% of your income.

As you can see, being able to make the down payment isn't enough. Lenders want to make sure that you'll be able to make your monthly payments. For this reason, they also look for job stability. Generally, they like for you to have been at the same job (or at least within the same industry) for two years or more.

As if all of this wasn't enough, you'll also have to come up with closing costs (items such as appraisals, insurance, and legal services which you generally pay at closing). Closing costs usually come to about 1-4% of the purchase price. Closing is when you, your attorney, the seller, the seller's attorney, and any real estate agents gather to formally turn over the property, in effect, close the deal.

MORTGAGE PROGRAMS

There are a number of mortgage programs specifically designed for first-time homebuyers and/or low-income families. These include Fannie Mae, Freddie Mac, and others. Some state-sponsored programs offer interest rates that are considerably lower than bank rates, and often require smaller down payments. Fannie Mae and Freddie Mac are programs sponsored by corporations created by the federal government. Their loans are made available through lending institutions. Ask your lender if you qualify.

COMING UP WITH THE DOWN PAYMENT

Sometimes your financial situation will qualify you for a mortgage on all counts—you have job stability, not too much debt, and you can certainly swing the monthly payments, but you just don't have the down payment sitting in the bank. What to do? Don't worry, there is still hope.

One possibility for some people is to ask their parents or other close relative for a gift. Lenders will not allow it to be a loan, since that will just add to your indebtedness. Lenders will want some kind of documentation that it is in fact a gift—that money can't just mysteriously appear in your bank account from one day to the next.

Another way relatives can help out is if they pledge their assets as collateral. The way it works is your relatives invest the equivalent of 20-30% of the loan amount with the lender's institution. You get a loan for the full amount of the purchase price. Your relatives are not giving up their assets; rather, they are posting them as a backup in case you default on the loan.

Another option is that you can tap your IRA up to $10,000 without penalty for a first-time home purchase.

If you have a 401(k) at work and your employer allows you to borrow from it with repayments coming out of your paycheck, this is another way to come up with the down payment.

TYPES OF MORTGAGES

Mortgages are typically for 30 years or 15 years. The interest on a mortgage can either be fixed or adjustable. With a fixed-rate mortgage, you pay the same rate of interest for the life of the loan. With an adjustable-rate mortgage, the rate of interest you pay can change at certain pre-determined intervals (for instance, six months and one year). Adjustable-rate mortgages usually have a lower initial rate than their fixed-rate counterparts. The problem is that an adjustable-rate mortgage is a bit of a gamble. You are betting that interest rates will drop; the lender is betting that they will rise. Shop around for the best rate. You can look on the Internet or your local newspaper to see what the different banks are offering. Look for any hidden fees (such as application fees). Also beware, sometimes lenders will want you to pay points. Points are payments you make at closing, in addition to the down payment and closing costs. Each point equals one percent of the loan amount. The general rule is when you pay points, the interest rate on your loan will be lower. Points can be advantageous if you plan to own the home for a long time.

TAX BENEFITS OF HOME OWNERSHIP

Owning a home presents a very nice tax benefit. Essentially, you can deduct your interest payments from your taxable income on your federal income tax. This can be substantial, especially in the first few years of mortgage payments when the majority of your payment is composed of interest. Also, any points you pay are tax deductible in the year you pay them.

Chapter 16
Tax Tips

THERE ARE SEVERAL THINGS YOU CAN DO TO MAKE TAXES LESS TAXING. Specifically, you want to (1) be sure that you are not declaring as "income" money that has come from non-taxable sources; (2) take advantage of as many credits as you are eligible for; and (3) deduct all those expenses for which you qualify. Follow these tips and you can significantly reduce the overall amount of tax you pay.

Sources of money that are not income

There are several sources of money that are not "income." Make sure you exclude these sources when reporting income. They include:

- **Gifts**
- **If you inherit money from a parent or grandparent, you don't pay any tax. The estate tax will be applied to the estate of the person who dies.**
- **Loans**
- **Life insurance proceeds**
- **Municipal bond interest**
- **Capital gains on the sale of your home up to $250,000 for single filers or $500,000 for joint filers**
- **Child support**
- **Property settlements in divorce proceedings**
- **Personal injury lawsuit settlements**
- **Workers' compensation payments**
- **Federal income tax refunds**
- **Scholarships and fellowships used for tuition, fees, books, and course equipment**

CREDITS

The IRS allows for certain credits, which reduce the total amount of tax you pay.

For some Gen Xers, the most significant of these credits is the Earned Income Tax Credit (EITC). According to the IRS, to claim the EITC on your 2000 tax return, you must meet all of the following rules:

1. **You must have earned income during the year.**
2. **Your earned income and modified adjusted gross income (AGI) must each be less than:**

- **$10,380 if you have no qualifying children, or**
- **$27,413 if you have one qualifying child, or**
- **$31,152 if you have more than one qualifying child.**
3. **Your investment income cannot be more than $2,400.**
4. **Your filing status can be any filing status EXCEPT married filing a separate return.**
5. **You cannot be a qualifying child of another person. If you are filing a joint return, neither you nor your spouse can be a qualifying child of another person.**
6. **Your qualifying child cannot be the qualifying child of another person whose modified AGI is more than yours.**

Another credit is the child tax credit. It works as follows:

For each qualifying child under the age of 17, you may be able to subtract $500 from your income tax. This applies for up to two children. You may be eligible for additional credits if you have three or more children and meet certain conditions.

Tax laws change, so stay on top of the changes to see how they affect you.

DEDUCTIONS

In addition to mortgage interest deductions (discussed in the chapter on buying a home) and IRA contributions (discussed in the IRA chapter), there are some other ways to lessen your tax bill. Here are some lesser-known areas.

MEDICAL EXPENSES

You can deduct your medical expenses, if they add up to 7.5% or more of your adjusted gross income for a single or family (joint) tax return. On a joint return the percentage is based on the total adjusted gross income of *both* the husband and wife. The difference between a single or family return is that you may have a larger adjusted gross income on a family tax return.

STUDENT LOAN INTEREST

The new student loan deduction offers the opportunity to write off up to $1,500 of interest paid in 1999 ($2,000 in 2000) on a loan used to pay college expenses of the taxpayer, the taxpayer's spouse, or the taxpayer's dependent. The deduction can be claimed for the first 60 months in which interest payments are required on the loan.

The deduction can be claimed regardless of whether you itemize your deductions. That's a big help to recent college grads who are paying off student loans and who usually don't have enough deductible expenses to itemize.

MOVING EXPENSES

If you move because of your job, you can deduct the expense so long as your new job location is at least 50 miles farther away from your old home than was your old job.

MISCELLANEOUS DEDUCTIONS

You can deduct miscellaneous itemized deductions only if they exceed 2% of your AGI. Here are some commonly overlooked items that can help you reach the mark:

DEDUCT YOUR JOB-HUNTING EXPENSES

If you hunt for a new job in the same line of work, you are eligible to deduct certain expenses that qualify under miscellaneous expenses. These include:

- **Expenses for resumes, cover letter, envelopes, and postage**
- **Fees for employment agencies**
- **Any magazines or newspapers you buy for classified ads**
- **Transportation to and from job interviews**
- **Long-distance calls to potential employers**
- **Out-of-town travel expenses if the trip is primarily to look for a new job**

INVESTMENT EXPENSES

Certain investment expenses can be deducted. These include:

- **Fees for investment advice**
- **The cost of books on investing**
- **Some investment-related travel**

HOME COMPUTER

If you buy a home computer and use it to help manage your investments, you may be able to write off part of the computer's cost as an investment expense. How much of the computer's cost can be deducted depends on how much time you use the computer to monitor your investments.

For example, if you bought a $2,500 computer system and use it 25 percent of the time to keep tabs on your investments, $625 of the computer's cost is eligible to be written off as a miscellaneous itemized expense. In most cases, the eligible costs must be written off over a five-year period.

CHARITABLE CONTRIBUTIONS

You can deduct charitable contributions as part of your itemized deductions. You can also deduct certain expenses related to volunteer work. For instance, you can deduct the cost of meals, lodging, and other travel expenses if you perform volunteer work away from home.

THE COST OF TAX PREPARATION

You can deduct the cost of preparing your taxes, including books, software, or a professional you pay to do your taxes for you.

A FINAL WORD ABOUT TAXES

A lot of folks get excited about receiving a big refund check after they file their tax return on or about April 15 each year. People will often brag about getting a hefty sum from the IRS every tax season. The truth is, these individuals are actually cheating themselves. If you are getting a refund come tax time, that simply means you've overpaid throughout the year—you've given Uncle Sam an interest-free loan, you might say. That's nothing to brag about.

Instead of getting a huge refund, see if you can adjust your withholdings at work accordingly so that you reduce your refund (in essence, reduce the "loan" you're giving Uncle Sam). This way, you'll actually have more money in your paycheck (instead of a lump-sum refund come tax time). You do this by filing a new W-4 form at work. File a new form if you get married, have a child, or buy a home, since these circumstances can change the amount of tax you owe. The IRS has a withholding allowance calculator on its website, www.irs.ustreas.gov.

CHAPTER 17
FINDING START-UP MONEY FOR YOUR BUSINESS

MANY GEN XERS ARE INTERESTED IN STARTING THEIR OWN BUSINESS, ESPECIALLY after experiencing life as a corporate worker. Here's a glimpse of how you can go about finding money for your new venture and what venture capitalists are looking to fund. Since most Gen Xers don't have a large sum of money to invest in a business, turning to outside sources of funding is the way to go. Below are some alternatives.

ANGEL INVESTORS, VENTURE CAPITALISTS, INCUBATORS

Angel investors are individuals with lots of money who are willing to provide start-up companies with funds in exchange for an expected large return on their investment. Angel investors look for companies with high growth potential, exciting products and/or services, and proven management.

Whereas angel investors are individuals, a venture capitalist is a professional business. Venture capitalists get money from what are called limited partners, for instance pension funds that need to diversify their risk. They have a small portion allotted for high-risk equity. VCs invest it for them in start-up firms.

Incubators nurture young firms. They provide hands-on management assistance, access to financing, and orchestrated exposure to critical business or technical support services. They also offer office services, access to equipment, flexible leases, and expandable space.

An incubation program's main goal is to produce successful graduates—businesses that are financially viable and freestanding when they leave the incubator usually in two to three years. Thirty percent of incubator clients typically graduate each year. According to the Impact of Incubator Investments Study, 1997, 87% of incubator graduates are still in business.

A GENERATION X STORY

iSTASH.COM

Shaun Manchand slept on a friend's futon while trying to get his company iStash.com off the ground. The 30-year-old is chief operating officer of the personal finance website for kids and teens. He and three other founders wrote the business plan in about a month in September 1999 and incorporated the company in December. Manchand, who has a master's degree in public policy from the University of Michigan, quit his job at Price Waterhouse Coopers on November 15, 1999 and lived off of savings.

"We had pre-identified a series of angel investors, let them know that the company was on the horizon, that there was a great management team in place, and that we would be ready to present to them a business plan by early winter," says Manchand.

Manchand wrote the business plan using research from the Internet and trade publications.

The 50 angel investors that invested in the company knew Manchand and the other founders through networking at events and through friends and family. The iStash crew was lucky. Their first round of financing netted $1.5 million.

WHERE TO FIND ANGEL INVESTORS

If you don't have individual contacts with angel investors, you can find them through an angel network, such as Yazam.com, AngelsForum.com, Angeltips.com, and Garage.com. Also look up Startups.com and click on Resource Locator for a list of other angel investor groups.

Angel networks are highly organized, very efficient, and offer value-added services like consulting for presentations and business plans. Once you locate an appropriate angel network, submit your executive summary and they will call if interested in introducing you to angels.

Venture capital investments increased 266% to $22.7 billion during the first quarter of the year 2000 and Internet-related companies captured the most investments, according to the National Venture Capital Association. About 1,557 companies received financing during the first quarter compared to only 851 companies in the first quarter of 1999.

WHAT VCs LOOK FOR IN BUSINESS PLANS

It's one of the great mysteries of the entrepreneurial universe: Just what are venture capitalists looking for?

Here's what they like, what they laugh at, and what they discard to help you refine your business plan:

THINGS THEY HATE

MOST COMMON FLAW

Robin Richards Donohoe, managing director of Draper International/ Draper Richards, San Francisco:

"The one thing that always drives us crazy is they don't give us their full resume. We're very much basing our money on the fact that this is a person who has showed a demonstration of good judgment throughout their lives, so we like to know everything.

"Another common flaw is they haven't done their homework on their competition in the marketplace; that is one of the ways we see how sharp a team is."

Darrell Williams, Chief Investment Officer of the Telecommunications Development Fund in Washington, D.C.: "Entrepreneurs pitch too many ideas that have little to do with their professional experience. For example, we get someone who is a retailer and they want to do a dot-com idea that has to do with business-to-business and their background has only to do with dealing with consumers."

Suzanne King, partner, New Enterprise Associates, Reston, Virginia: "The most common flaw is trying to put everything in the business plan plus the kitchen sink. What I want in the first page of your business plan is a succinct description of what you do, what problem you solve, and why anybody cares."

WHAT THEY SEE TOO MUCH OF

Ms. Donohoe: Niche Web sites.

Wyc Grousbeck, general partner with Highland Capital Partners, Boston: Medical billing.

John Neis, partner at the firm Venture Investors, Madison, Wisconsin: Redundant dot-coms. "It's particularly evident in business-to-consumer space where we feel there is not adequate differentiation or meaningful barriers to competitive entry."

Patty Abramson, managing director, Women's Growth Capital Fund, Washington, D.C.: "I think we see too much of slapping a retail store idea with Internet presence and assuming it is an Internet company."

Venetia Kontogouris, managing director, Trident Capital, Westport, Connecticut: "How many plans can we have about health care and diseases?"

SILLIEST IDEAS THEY'VE BEEN PITCHED

Mr. Williams: A proposal to build a full-scale replica of The Starship Enterprise.

Mr. Neis: A flying bike. "This individual wanted to create a human-powered helicopter which obviously technically would be virtually impossible and secondly no market for it. But you know we all run into our crazies."

Doug Morriss, chairman of Gryphon Investments, St. Louis: A dirt farm. "The business was attempting to smelt dirt. They were trying to go into gold-mining companies and acquire the mineral rights for these places and actually scoop up the remains of these things and put them through some gigantic incinerator that was going to smelt away the leftover gold."

Ms. Donohoe: "There was a guy from Turkey who had written poems and songs for Princess Diana. . . . He wanted us to finance the publishing of these songs and his poetry, and he wanted us to also finance a Web site dedicated to Princess Diana. We've had a candle play—a pitch to have everything about candles on one Web site. We've had a Lobster B-to-B play, where they would sell lobsters online."

Ms. Kontogouris: Putting a semi conductor chip in a dog. "You know, tracking your dog if your dog gets lost. . . . I thought it very peculiar and different first of all because it can be cruel to the animal. Second of all, if the chip runs out of battery your dog gets lost anyway."

THINGS THEY LIKE

BEST RECENT BUSINESS CONCEPT

Linda Powers, managing director with Toucan Capital in Bethesda, Maryland: A cinema project in Prague. "Galaxy Cinema was a project that took a former Bolshevik cultural center and very rapidly transformed it. It was the absolute first mover to market in the whole region and this is a region where the demand for entertainment is off the charts and the supply is totally absent."

Ms. Abramson: "The best business concept I've seen is a concept that allows a person faced with information overload to organize and categorize all the information that they have and all the things they want to know about all these subjects."

Ms. King: "From my portfolio of companies right now the best one that stands out in my mind is an optical networking company and the local access space." (This, she says, will help transport data high speed to homes and small businesses, which are not hindered by slow, old local phone lines.)

Mr. Williams: A roll-up in the transportation business. "This was a combination of passenger travel in limousine and small bus service and this company had a license from the Department of Transportation to do a lot of transport that most companies of that size did not have. They would be providing transportation service for individuals through their limited sedan services and maybe providing bus services, short distance bus services on prescribed routes."

WHAT THEY'D LIKE TO SEE MORE OF

Ms. Powers: "Anything that you could visualize somebody using every day. We always look very closely at that. The person who thought up the paper-clip, that is the kind of thing we love because that's the kind of thing that over the long run is going to be enormous because it's something people will use every single day."

Mr. Grousbeck: A fantastic management team. "I look for great experience and that the plan has been referred by somebody that Highland knows well. It's that personal reference. I really can't stress that enough."

Mr. Williams: Ditto. "I look for the ability or the background of the management relative to the idea that they are proposing. So if management's background and experience is consistent and they've had some track record of success with what it is they are proposing, that will get my instant attention."

Ms. Donohoe: Ditto again. "I'd say what we miss the most is a good team and a really fleshed-out business plan."

Mr. Neis: A novel innovation that really provides a distinct competitive advantage. "We look for those nonlinear technical breakthroughs that kind of upsets the dynamics of a marketplace and we look for an opportunity for a patented position that would enable a company to have a sustainable competitive advantage."

Ms. Abramson: "I think now I'd like to see more diversity in business plans. We tend to see mostly everything in the Internet space."

A GENERATION X STORY

THE GEEK FACTORY

Peter Shankman needed money to start his own Internet public relations business, but he didn't want to go into anymore debt to do it. So, in August 1998, he came up with the novel idea of selling t-shirts. But not just any t-shirt.

"The movie *Titanic* was coming out on video and I had no money, but I knew I needed money to incorporate. I took my rent money for September and I had 500 t-shirts printed up that read 'It Sank, Get Over It.' I went to Times Square and I figured if I could sell 180, I would break even," says Shankman.

The 28-year-old wound up selling 500 in fewer than six hours, making a whopping $5,000.

"I needed more money to pay off my credit cards than I needed to actually start the company. I needed in total maybe ten grand just to buy a couple of new computers and just to pay off some bills," he said.

The Boston University graduate telephoned a reporter at *USA Today* who asked Shankman if he was selling the t-shirts online.

"I said 'oh, yeah, sure.' I then built a website. She ran the story the next day and I got tons of exposure from that. The story ran on CNN, [in] *Chicago Tribune, New York Times, Entertainment Weekly, People, Newsday,* and *Time.* From there I sold thousands of them, which funded the company," say Shankman.

The first year, Shankman operated his public relations business, the Geek factory, out of his Manhattan apartment until he started getting calls for more work. "It was an amount of work versus lack of sleep ratio and the sleep was losing, and so I hired one person in December of 1999. That was my first hire and that is when I got my first office and that now has turned into seven people and a bigger office."

Shankman's Geek Factory counts Internet firms such as Mondas.com and RegisterFree.com among its clients. In 1999, the firm had revenues of $100,000. In 2000, Shankman said the firm had revenues of more than a million dollars.

WORKING WITH INCUBATORS

Most incubators take a cut in return for the services they provide to start-up businesses. The problem occurs when they take more of the company than what their services are worth. In some cases, incubators have taken up to 85% equity in a company.

"Really the decision to raise money or to go into an incubator is a financial transaction where each side is making an estimate of the value that they are contributing and the value that they are receiving. I think for a company that is considering going into an incubator they need to take a closer look at what it is an incubator is providing," says Justin Segal, co-founder and vice president of corporate development at Startups.com in California.

Among the things an incubator provides is funding, strategy management experience, product development, consulting, and operations such as physical infrastructure, facilities, office space, phones and conference rooms, and relief of stress, which is a psychological benefit.

People feel that if there is an incubator, they don't have to worry so much but getting into an incubator may be difficult. There is a public and private face. You can submit a business plan through the Internet and hope they call or perhaps you know someone who can hand deliver your plan to an executive.

"The way it works more frequently is that there is a personal relationship. The founder or the entrepreneur will know somebody who has a connection to an incubator or the venture fund or the angel investor or the angel network," says Segal.

As an entrepreneur looking for funding, your time is best spent developing relationships with people rather than submitting your business plan all over the Internet. Join a couple of organizations and network. In New York City, there's the New York New Media Association and in California, there's the Churchill Group. In Boston, check out the Massachusetts Interactive Media Counsel.

"If you are an entrepreneur and you don't have good networking skills, it is significantly more difficult to raise funding," says Segal.

TechSpace falls into the incubator category. It receives ten percent of equity of a company that is admitted but TechSpace is different in that it pays money in exchange for the ten percent.

"At TechSpace, we have a host of a la carte services which are kind of accelerator services. They will help grow your business at a quicker speed. People have access to recruitment, marketing, branding, and business plan writing but at competitive fees. They pay for the space, they pay for the services, and they pay for the technology," says Debra Larsen, president and CEO of TechSpace.

Coming into TechSpace you have to be self-financed, have received angel financing, or received a round or two of venture financing.

Typically, when working with an incubator you give up a significant portion of your company and they help to provide that speed to market. For example, you may give 40% in exchange for space and services.

At companies like TechSpace, you have the ability to start a business at cheaper costs and you get plugged into a network of other companies. The downside is you may become accustomed to all the services and not want to leave the site.

"Entrepreneurs get soft because TechSpace provides so many services so easily that when they have to leave, they are not used to having to find space and doing their own technology," says Larsen.

Once admitted into TechSpace, expect to pay about $600 to $700 a month per employee for office space, technology services, and administrative services.

It sounds like a good deal but if you are secretive about your business, TechSpace might not be the place for you. "If you think someone is going to steal your idea, this wouldn't be the right environment because it is about open doors and collaboration and synergy," says Larsen.

Some people may think it's too expensive but you do get what you pay for.

"You could set up card tables in some space down in the East Village if you could find it. You could do that. It is not the most professional. It's not the easiest way to attract employees or other venture capitalists but some people really want to be cheap and easy with their money in the beginning. For those people this is not the right environment," says Larsen. "This is professional space. It's hip, it's cool, it's fun but it is also not the garage."

A GENERATION X STORY

FLOOZ.COM

Robert Levitan attributes his company's success in New York City to a "karmic boomerang" in Manhattan's emerging Silicon Alley. Founded in December 1998, in just two years, the private company had grown from 25 people to 92 people and from 800 square feet of office space to 12,000 square feet.

The CEO and founder of Flooz.com says an example of karmic boomerang is people volunteering to help him found the online gift currency company that boasts Whoopi Goldberg as its spokesperson.

"I know a lot of people in New York, and when I left iVillage there were a lot of people who wanted to help. They said if there is anything we can do to help just let me know. I didn't realize how well known I was and how much support I had inside the New York Internet community," says Levitan.

Flooz sells web-based gift vouchers that are sent by e-mail and can be used in 100 stores online, which means that Levitan spends a lot of time maintaining relationships with retailers, online distributors, and online greeting card providers.

The company has received increased demand from corporate clients. As a result, Flooz started a site called Flooz for Business. More than 60% of the company's business is corporate in terms of gross sales. Levitan estimates that it will grow to around 70%. In addition to catering to corporate clients, Flooz is launching in Britain after talking with some 15 retailers in the UK, including Harrods and Tower Records.

Heady stuff for a former small-time entrepreneur who attended public school in New York City and once owned a video company in Durham, North Carolina.

Levitan chose to stay in New York's Internet community dubbed "Silicon Alley" rather than move to San Francisco's Silicon Valley because he wanted to be a big fish in a small pond.

"If I had gone to San Francisco there still would have been support but not at the same level. I was a pioneer here but I would not be considered a pioneer out there," says Levitan.

The 39-year-old says securing Ms. Goldberg as spokesperson is also an example of karmic boomerang.

"We were talking with lots of agents and celebrities and managers and it turns out that there was a woman over at William Morris [who] had heard of Flooz [who] had a friend [who] worked here [who] had heard of me and was familiar with what I did at iVillage. It didn't look like we were going to get Whoopi until this woman at William Morris suggested that Whoopi and I should speak on the phone. Whoopi and I spoke on the phone and she just got excited," says Levitan.

The Duke University graduate is one of the old school members of Silicon Alley. He is one of the founders of iVillage, one of the first Internet companies based in New York City. Levitan founded it along with Candace Carpenter and Nancy Evans in 1995 while working as consultants with AOL.

He was urged by officials at the New York New Media Association to base Flooz in Manhattan rather than dashing to San Francisco.

"They said, 'Robert, it is really important that people who are first-generation New York Internet entrepreneurs stay in New York and do another start-up because what made Silicon Valley so successful was all these computer companies had second- and third-generation entrepreneurs who started Internet companies and New York never really had that,' " says Levitan.

After four years of building iVillage, Levitan branched out on his own with partner Spencer Waxman to found Flooz. They each put in about $100,000 of their own money before approaching angel investors and venture capitalists.

"We immediately did an angel round and we found 30 people who were interested in investing. We raised about three million dollars of angel money in the winter of 1998. In January, February, and March of 1999 and then in July 1999, we did a round of financing with some venture capitalists and that was about 13.5 million dollars. We took the three million from the angels and the 13.5 million from the venture capitalist, and converted all of that to equity," he said.

Levitan wasn't just at the right place at the right time back in 1995; he's worked very hard to keep his new company afloat. He says his best attributes are passion and sincerity.

"I think people trust me as a leader. I would like to think I am intelligent but there are a lot of people who are in this business [who] are a lot smarter than me. It's fun and I find it intellectually stimulating. To me it is not work. I would do it for free. You just have to be passionate, creative, and stimulating and I think that leads to success. If you are doing something that you find stimulating and interesting, you are going to be successful at it," says Levitan.

APPENDIX A
RISK TOLERANCE PROFILE

The following tasks or questions are designed to help you understand how you feel about putting your investments at risk. There are no "right" answers to these questions. The correct responses are totally based on your feelings. They provide a beginning point for our future discussions about risk and loss.[*]

PART I: Select the *one* answer that most resembles your attitude toward investing:

- ☐ I cannot afford any possible loss of principal regardless of potential return.
- ☐ While unable to risk my principal, I want more income than CDs would pay.
- ☐ If I can get high yields from bonds, it's not worth suffering through the ups and downs of the stock market.
- ☐ Although stocks will earn better returns than other types of securities, I will forego some future gains in order to earn a steady stream of income.

[*]The material on pages 145-157 courtesy The Arkansas Financial Group, © 1999, All rights reserved.

☐ I need current, dependable income, but I consider it essential to have some monies invested where they have the potential for growth.

☐ I believe in the power of compounding income and the potential for gain from stocks and want a combination of the two.

☐ Solid companies in stable businesses should give good results with a level of risk I can tolerate.

☐ Smaller is better in the long run. Small companies' stocks may be more volatile but will reward me with the best long-term results.

☐ I believe that I can select good companies to own and enjoy the thrill and challenge of ferreting out attractive stocks.

☐ Higher risk investors will generally earn higher returns, and I want the potential of higher returns even if it means experiencing significant losses for extended periods of time.

PART II: **Five portfolios are depicted below showing their annual percentage return over five successive years. If *all* of your investments were invested using one of these strategies, which one would you prefer? (circle one)**

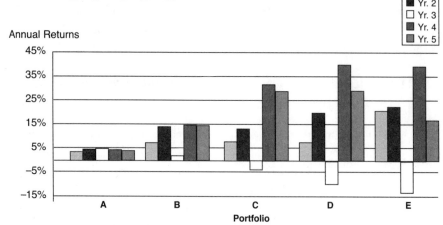

PART III: **Assume you have been presented with two sets of decisions about an investment option. How you got the money or how much you invested is not material. The emphasis is on the two different sets of outcomes. For each of these two decisions, check the option you would choose:**

Decision 1—Choose between:

☐ a. A sure gain of $25,000

☐ b. A 25% chance of winning $100,000 and a 75% chance of winning nothing

Decision 2—Choose between:

☐ a. A sure loss of $75,000

☐ b . A 75% chance of losing $100,000 and a 25% chance of losing nothing

PART IV: Portfolio Characteristics

This section lets you tell us what you value in a portfolio. We have listed the five characteristics any investment or portfolio can reflect. Identify the importance you place on each characteristic by circling the number that best indicates your set of priorities. Let 5 indicate great importance and 1 indicate little importance.

Use two sets of constraints in your scoring. First, Safety of Principal and Growth should total six. Second, make the necessary adjustments so that the total for the five characteristics adds up to 14. This means that you should allocate the remaining eight points among the last three characteristics. If you have questions or observations about any of the characteristics, please note those in the comments section.

Characteristic	Degree of Importance	Comments
Safety of Principal	1 2 3 4 5	
Growth	1 2 3 4 5	
Current Income	1 2 3 4 5	
Liquidity	1 2 3 4 5	
Tax Reduction	1 2 3 4 5	
Total (should be 14)		

PART V: General Portfolio Objective: Which statement best describes your investment objective? (circle one)

a. **Capital Preservation**—The safety of investments is most important. Even though the returns may be low, the risk level should mean virtually no chance of losing my money.

b. **Income**—My main concern is receiving income with some modest growth of my assets.

c. **Growth & Income**—My main concern is with the growth of my portfolio with only a small emphasis on portfolio income. Investments could include stocks, bonds, and cash for diversification and risk management.

d. **Growth**—My only concern is with the growth of my portfolio, even if this means that my portfolio will experience more "ups and downs" during market cycles.

e. **Aggressive Growth**—I *really* want my portfolio to grow aggressively. While this may result in violent swings in value (including periods of major losses), I want to "beat the market" over time.

PART VI: Return and Risk Expectations

What would you consider to be a "reasonable annual rate of return" after your money has been invested over a long period of time? _____%

Your tolerance for risk can best be described as:

☐   I can tolerate more than one year of negative absolute returns through difficult phases in a market cycle.

☐   I can tolerate two or three quarters of negative absolute returns through difficult phases in a market cycle.

☐   I can tolerate infrequent, very moderate losses through difficult phases in a market cycle.

What is the maximum loss (or minimum rate of return) you could tolerate in any one year, expressed as a % of your portfolio (for example: 2%, 0%, -2%, -5%, -10%)? _____ %

PART VII: Investment Objective Analyzer

Please select the answer that fits you the best for each question, marking the appropriate box. There are no "right" or "wrong" answers. Everyone has his or her own level of investment knowledge and experience, as well as the level of risk he or she is willing to take.

1. What is your age? _____

2. What do you expect to be your next major expenditure?

☐   Buying a house

☐   Paying for a college education

☐   Capitalizing a new business

☐   Providing for retirement

3. When do you expect to use the bulk of the money in your investments?

☐   At any time now . . . so a high level of liquidity is important

☐   Probably in the next 1-5 years

☐ In 6-10 years
☐ Probably in 11-20 years
☐ In more than 20 years

4. Over the next several years, you expect your annual income to:

☐ Stay about the same
☐ Grow moderately
☐ Grow substantially
☐ Decrease moderately
☐ Decrease substantially

5. Due to a general market correction, one of your investments loses 14% of its value a short time after you buy it. What do you do?

☐ Sell the investment so you won't have to worry if it continues to decline.
☐ Hold on to it and wait for it to climb back up.
☐ Buy more of the same investment . . . because at the new low price, it looks even better than when you bought it.

6. Which of these plans would you choose for your investment dollars?

☐ You'd go for maximum diversity, dividing your portfolio among a large variety of investments, including those ranging from highest return/greatest risk to lowest return/lowest risk.
☐ You're concerned with simplicity, so you would simply divide your portfolio between two investments, each with above average return and risk.
☐ You would put your investment dollars into the investment with the highest rate of return and most risk.

7. Assuming you're investing in a stock mutual fund, which one do you choose?

☐ A fund with companies with potential to make significant technological breakthroughs, and whose stocks are still at their low initial offering prices

☐ A fund that only invests in established, well-known companies that have a potential for continued growth

☐ A fund devoted to "blue chip," highly diversified stocks that pay dividends

8. Assuming you're investing in only one bond, which bond do you choose?

☐ A "junk bond" that pays a higher rate than the next two bonds, but also gives you the least sense of security with regard to a possible default

☐ A "treasury bond" that pays the lowest interest of these first three bonds but is backed by the United States Government

☐ The bond of a well-established company that pays a rate of interest somewhere between the first two bonds

☐ A "tax-free bond" since minimizing taxes is a major concern

9. Indicate the importance you place on actually receiving income from your investments right now:

☐ Essential and must be known

☐ Essential but willing to accept uncertainty about the amount

☐ Important but other factors also influence

☐ A modest amount is desirable

☐ I don't currently need income from my investments

10. Your advisor expects inflation to return and suggests that you invest in "hard assets" such as gold, oil and gas, or real estate, which have historically provided a hedge against inflation. Your only financial assets are long-term bonds. What do you do?

☐ Ignore the advice and hold onto the bonds.

☐ Sell the bonds, putting half the proceeds into hard assets and the other half into money market funds.

☐ Sell the bonds and put all of the proceeds into hard assets.

☐ Sell the bonds, not only put all of the proceeds into hard assets, but also borrow additional money so you can buy even more hard assets.

11. **Your friend is starting a new consulting business and has given you the opportunity to invest. The chance of the business surviving and returning your investment is only 10%. But, if the operation is successful, you could earn 40% on your investment. How much do you invest?**

 ☐ Nothing at all

 ☐ One month's salary

 ☐ Three months' salary

 ☐ Six months' salary

12. **You have just reached the $10,000 plateau on a popular TV game show. Now you must choose between quitting with the $10,000 in hand or betting the entire $10,000 on one of three alternative scenarios. Which one do you choose?**

 ☐ The $10,000 . . . you take the money and run!

 ☐ You win $20,000 if you guess right on the flip of a coin.

 ☐ You win $50,000 if you guess the right box out of five boxes.

 ☐ You win $100,000 if you guess the right number between 1 and 10.

"THOUGHT QUESTIONS"

How much would you like to have uninvested and available for emergencies?

_____

Are there factors or conditions that you feel would affect your life expectancy more positively or negatively than what might be considered normal?

_____

_____

How would you characterize the stability of: (1) your industry,
(2) your company, and (3) your income?   _____

_____

By what percentage do you feel your earnings will increase or decrease annually over the next five years? _____% What are the key factors that will have a bearing on this? _____

_____

To what extent are you pleased with your ability to manage and shelter your income from taxes? _____

_____

To what extent are you pleased with the diversification and performance of your portfolio? _____

_____

What's the best investment and the worst investment you have ever made?

Best: _____

_____

Worst: _____

_____

Are there any investments you would be reluctant to sell (for past performance, family, or social reasons)? If yes, which ones?

_____

_____

Are there any investments you would be reluctant to buy or own (for reasons similar to the previous question)? If yes, which ones?

_____

_____

What have you accomplished in your financial life that makes you feel good about yourself? _____

_____

_____

What, if anything, about your finances causes you to lie awake at night?

_____

_____

What are the things in your financial life you wish you had done differently, or actually cause you to feel a bit embarrassed to discuss?

_____

_____

What financial activities are you expecting our firm to carry out for you?

_____

_____

What financial activities are you going to prefer to carry out yourself?

_____

_____

Scoring the Risk Profile

The 1 to 10 Scale (Part I):

These questions are simply arrayed in order of increasing willingness to accept risk. Another way to look at it is to ask yourself: "On a scale of one to ten, with one being squeaky conservative and ten being metaphysically wild and crazy, how would you score your willingness to accept risk?" Take the answer and divide by 2. Then convert to a portfolio type as follows: 5 = Aggressive Growth; 4 = Growth; 3 = Growth & Income; 2 = Income; 1 = Capital Preservation.

Portfolio Objective (Parts II, V, and VII):

Your portfolio objective is measured using three methods. Part V labels and directly describes the five general objectives. Part II graphically presents portfolios that reflect the likely behavior of those five objectives. Part VII allows you to infer your portfolio objective.

Question	A	B	C	D	E
1.	3	2	1		
2.	1	2	3	2	
3.	1	2	3	4	5
4.	3	4	5	2	1
5.	1	3	5		
6.	1	3	5		
7.	5	3	1		
8.	5	1	3	1	
9.	1	2	3	4	5
10.	1	3	4	5	
11.	1	2	4	5	
12.	1	2	4	5	

Total Score	Maximum Loss/ Minimum Return	Risk Type
10–16	3.0%	Capital Preservation
17–24	1.0%	Income
25–36	–1.0%	Growth & Income
37–46	–3.5%	Growth
47 +	–6.0%	Aggressive Growth

Modified Kahneman–Tversky Test (Part III):

Decision 1	Decision 2	Risk Preference
a	a	Risk Averse
a	b	Loss Averse
b	a	Disciplined Risk Taker
b	b	Risk Taker

Constrained Portfolio Characteristics (Part IV):

The most important score in this part is the Degree of Importance placed on Growth. Take the score for Growth and convert to a portfolio type as follows: 5 = Aggressive Growth; 4 = Growth; 3 = Growth & Income; 2 = Income; 1 = Capital Preservation.

Stated Portfolio Risk and Return Expectations (Part VI):

While this part is straight forward, the answers should be consistent with the other answers since this is the "bogey" to which you will hold your portfolio.

Once the scoring is completed, summarize in order to see inconsistencies. For example, your summary might look like this:

I.	1–10 Scale	Growth & Income
II.	Chart	Growth & Income
IV.	Characteristics	Income
V.	Objective	Income
VII.	Inferred	Growth & Income
III.	K/T Test	Loss Avoider
VI.	Expectations:	

Appendix B

Internet Resources

Apartments and Roommates

Apartments for Rent Online

Offers more than 60,000 apartment listings, many with floor plans, photographs, and virtual tours.

http://www.forrent.realpage.com

Easyroommate

A nationwide roommate matching service.

http://www.easyroommate.chuckiii.com/index.cfm?ac=chuckiii

AUTOS

EDMUNDS

Offers new car prices and used car prices as well as auto reviews.

http://www.edmunds.com/

AUTOBYTEL.COM

A leading site for buying or selling a vehicle, shopping for insurance, or virtually any auto-related product.

http://www.autobytel.com/

KELLEY BLUE BOOK

A good place to go for pricing on new and used vehicles, buying a car, getting insurance, etc.

http://www.kbb.net/

CAR-BUYING TIPS

Advice on automobile buying and leasing. Claims to reveal "every single dealer scam known to mankind."

http://www.carbuyingtips.com/

BANKING

BANKRATE.COM

Here you'll find rates from more than 4,000 financial institutions across the 50 states. Everything from auto loans and certificates of deposit to savings accounts and home equity loans.

http://www.bankrate.com

WINGSPAN BANK

Don't look for branch locations of this bank; it's Internet-only.

http://www.wingspan.com

CAREER/JOBS

TEMP-JOBS.NET

Offers thousands of listings of temporary jobs nationwide. Also lets you post your resume, look into career fairs, and more.

http://www.temp-jobs.net/

HEADHUNTER.NET

A vast database listing more than 250,000 jobs in a wide variety of fields. It's also a place to post your resume.

http://www.headhunter.net

CAREERBUILDER

Billing itself as a "mega job search," Careerbuilder searches more than 75 sites for jobs. It also includes a Layoff Survival Kit.

http://www.careerbuilder.com

MONSTER.COM

One of the best-known job search sites, monster.com has over half a million job postings. You can e-mail your resume to thousands of recruiters instantly.

http://www.monsterboard.com

SALARY.COM

This site features a salary wizard that tells you the going salary for a given job within a selected state or region. It also provides advice and career resources.

http://www.salary.com

TELECOMMUTING JOBS

Want to work from home? Here's the place to find your dream (telecommuting) job.

http://www.tjobs.com

HOME BUYING

HOMES.COM

A comprehensive resource for finding homes and apartments, real estate agents and brokers, home services, mortgages, and much more.

http://www.homes.com

REALTOR.COM

This one-stop shop provides resources for finding the right neighborhood, buying a home, moving, decorating, lawn and garden needs, etc.

http://www.realtor.com

IOWN.COM

This site makes it easy to shop for a mortgage, buy a new home, refinance your existing home, or take out a home equity loan.

http://www.iown.com

INSURANCE

QUOTESMITH.COM

Quotesmith.com is a great way to get quotes from more than 300 companies on all kinds of insurance—life, homeowners, medical, dental, and much more.

http://www.quotesmith.com

INVESTING

NEW YORK STOCK EXCHANGE

If you can't get to the floor of the exchange itself, visit the home page of the New York Stock Exchange (NYSE).

http://www.nyse.com

NATIONAL ASSOCIATION OF REAL ESTATE INVESTMENT TRUSTS

NAREIT Online is the Internet home of the National Association of Real Estate Investment Trusts. The site provides good information about investing in REITs and publicly traded real estate.

http://www.nareit.com

RETIRE ON YOUR TERMS

The National Association for Variable Annuities sponsors this site which provides information and resources relating to annuities.

http://www.retireonyourterms.com

ARTNET.COM

If you are looking for fine art, a good place to start is Artnet.com, which allows you to search artists, galleries, and exhibitions.

http://www.artnet.com

ICOLLECTOR.COM

This site is dedicated to trading antiques, fine art, and collectibles. It represents more than 300 auction houses and 650 dealers and galleries.

http://www.icollector.com

MAXFUNDS.COM

Helping people pick better funds is the goal of Maxfunds.com. This site provides valuable information you can use to make better investing decisions.

http://www.maxfunds.com

CHARLES SCHWAB & CO.

The Internet home of one of the leading brokerage firms.

http://www.schwab.com

MORNINGSTAR.COM

A good starting point to get news and information concerning stocks, funds, and investing in general.

http://www.morningstar.com

THE KELLER GROUP

The Keller Group is an investment advisory firm, which provides investment management and financial planning on a fee-only basis.

http://kellerinvestment.com

YAHOO FINANCE VISION

Yahoo Finance Vision could be described as interactive television on the Internet. It provides live market coverage as well as interviews with leading experts in personal finance and investing. Viewers get to ask questions of the guests.

http://vision.yahoo.com

USA Today—Money

The Money Section of *USA Today's* Internet edition is terrific not just for news, but also for investment research and personal finance tools.

http://www.usatoday/money/mfront.htm

Money and Love

Premarital Agreement

That's right, you guessed it, a website dedicated to premarital (prenuptial) agreements. You can get advice as well as download free, do-it-yourself agreements.

http://premaritalagreement.com

Saving Money

Coupons.com

Why sit there clipping coupons, when you can print them from your computer? Coupons.com offers discounts and freebies for nearly everything under the sun.

http://www.coupons.com

PRICELINE.COM

The "name your own price" website for discounts on a variety of products, including groceries, long-distance telephone service, cars, and airline tickets.

http://www.priceline.com

LOWER MY BILLS

Ever feel that you pay too much on your monthly bills? Ever wonder if you are getting the best deal? LowerMyBills.com lets you comparison shop for things such as long-distance phone service, credit cards, insurance, Internet service, utilities, and more.

http://lowermybills.com

TAXES

INTERNAL REVENUE SERVICE

What better place to get tax information than from the IRS.

http://www.irs.ustreas.gov

TRAVEL

TRAVELOCITY.COM

Save yourself a trip to the local travel agent. Find low rates on vacation packages, hotels, cruises, rental cars, and flights on Tracelocity.com.

http://www.travelocity.com

LIBERTY TRAVEL

Liberty Travel is one of the oldest and most respected travel agencies around, with more than 50 years of experience. Libertytravel.com is its online presence.

http://www.libertytravel.com

EXPEDIA.COM

Expedia is an online travel service for flights, hotels, car rentals, and vacation packages, and also offers travel-related news and advice.

http://www.expedia.com

EUROVACATIONS.COM

As the name implies, this site specializes in travel to European destinations.

http://www.eurovacations.com

WHERE NEXT

For those who find travel guide books to be stale and out of date, this site provides the perfect alternative or complement. Wherenext.com prides itself in providing up-to-date and relevant information on a wide number of destinations.

http://www.wherenext.com

CONTIKI

Contiki offers worldwide vacations for 18- to 35-year-olds.

http://www.contiki.com

ONETRAVEL.COM

OneTravel.com's slogan says it all, "Low Price. Great Advice. All in One."

http://www.onetravel.com

TRIP.COM

Among its many travel services, this site offers a weekly newsletter via e-mail.

http://www.trip.com

TOM PARSON'S BEST FARES.COM

Members of bestfares.com receive special deals on travel both nationally and internationally.

http://www.bestfares.com

Cheaptickets.com

Buy cheap plane tickets, but some conditions apply.

www.cheaptickets.com

Miscellaneous Resources

Social Security Administration

Everything you ever wanted to know about social security is here.

http://www.ssa.gov

The Longevity Game

An interactive lifestyle and health awareness quiz, to get a general idea of how long you may live past retirement. Presented by Northwestern Mutual.

http://www.northwesternmutual.com/nmcom/NM/longevitygameintro/toolbox—calculator—longevitygameintro—longevity_intro

GetSmart.com

GetSmart.com bills itself as a financial marketplace. Here you can get mortgage loans, credit cards, debt consolidation, online bill paying, car loans, and other services.

http://www.getsmart.com

ABOUT THE AUTHOR

Juliette Fairley is a personal finance writer, professional speaker, and money coach. She has written for *Investor's Business Daily, USA Today, The New York Times,* and *Financial Planning* magazine about personal finance topics. Miss Fairley has been featured on CNBC, MSNBC, Curtis Court, Good Day New York, and Bloomberg Television.

Her first book, *Money Talks* was published in 1998, and her second book, *CliffsNotes on Mutual Funds* appeared in 1999. Charles Schwab sponsored Miss Fairley's first book tour to six cities.

The author graduated from Columbia University's Graduate School of Journalism in 1991 and lived and worked in Paris, France as an English-language translator. She attended the University of Wisconsin's Graduate School of Banking in Madison. She is a member of the New York New Media Association, the Author's Guild, the American Society of Journalists and Authors, and the New York Financial Writers Association.

A Gen Xer, Miss Fairley is a spokesperson for the Ford Motor Company. She is a sought after public speaker and can be booked for keynotes and workshops. Call 212-714-7723 or visit her website at www.AboutJuliette.com.

Index

*Page numbers appearing in italics refer to tables.